12.95

Armchair BASIC

An Absolute Beginner's Guide to Programming in BASIC

Annie Fox and David Fox

Osborne/McGraw-Hill
Berkeley, California

Published by
Osborne/McGraw-Hill
2600 Tenth Street
Berkeley, California 94710
U.S.A.

For information on translations and book distributors
outside of the U.S.A., please write to Osborne/McGraw-
Hill at the above address.

**ARMCHAIR BASIC: AN ABSOLUTE BEGINNER'S GUIDE TO
PROGRAMMING IN BASIC**

  4567890 DODO 8987654
ISBN 0-931988-92-6
Cover and text illustration by Randee S. Fox
Text design by KLT van Genderen

DEDICATION

For my mother, Martha Larris, with love

-ALF

To my literary mentor, Mitchell Waite

-DBF

ACKNOWLEDGMENTS

This book has been brewing for years. Every Tuesday night, in the course of teaching our Beginning BASIC class, we wondered if we would ever have a book that could be a companion to beginners who were starting on their quest for computer information. We finally realized that we should write the book ourselves. We did, and we'd like to acknowledge the following people for their significant contributions to making *Armchair BASIC* a reality.

Randee Fox-Williams for lightening the cover and the pages within with her wonderful, waggish, and whimsical illustrations.

Mary Cron, Kerin Deeley, Scot Kamins, Les Overlock, Ann Schalit, and Michelle Virzi for their careful and thoughtful review of our manuscript and warm encouragement.

Lynda Whitley of Cray Research for information on the CRAY X-MP super computer.

Phyllis Zale of Novato Public Library, who really was tireless in her efforts to help us track down a portrait of Charles Babbage.

Barbara Kelly for her endless patience and good humor while babysitting for Jessica.

Jessica Fox for being such a good girl during all the hours that Mommy and Daddy were busy working on this book.

Medea, our faithful hound, who provided moral support and foot-warming services while she slept under the word processor.

And, finally, the thousands of people with their thousands of questions who took our Beginning BASIC course at Marin Computer Center: their desire to learn served as the impetus for this book.

Annie Fox
David Fox

CONTENTS

PREFACE

In 1976, when we first became curious about computers, it was quite an undertaking to teach ourselves about them. We two intelligent people found that poring through technical manuals was about as easy as reading a Martian manuscript without the aid of a dictionary or an interpreter. What we needed was some *introductory* material that assumed the reader knew nothing, but back then there was a mere thimbleful of information for beginners. We saw that a microcomputer geyser was about to erupt. So in 1977, to do our part in filling the informational void, we opened the Marin Computer Center, the first public access microcomputer facility whose sole purpose was to accommodate the beginner.

The technology has come a long way since those days, and so has the demand for computer information on the part of "everyday people." Today, most of us are beginning to see the potential usefulness of microcomputers, and are busily dreaming up ways in which we can personally benefit from them. To best take advantage of the newest servant of humankind, we all need to be educated. We don't all need to become computer programmers, but it is essential that we have enough knowledge about computers to feel comfortable with them. We ought to become familiar enough with their capabilities and limitations to be able to use them in any desired capacity. In other words, we all should become "computer literate" in this Computer Age.

Toward this end, we have written *Armchair BASIC,* "An Absolute Beginner's Guide to Programming in BASIC." You'll become familiar with much of the befuddling terminology that accompanies the field and learn enough of the basics of BASIC (a very popular programming language) to be able to converse very competently with a computer if the occasion ever arises.

Armchair BASIC is designed for people who have no prior experience with computers and have recently purchased one, or are thinking about it. Even without access to a computer, you'll be able to read this book cover to cover and learn how to program in BASIC, because no hands-on experience is required to understand the concepts presented here. (If you do have a computer, the program examples in this book can be used with the BASIC for any computer.) *Armchair BASIC* will enable you to feel comfortable with computers, work with them confidently, and teach someone else (coworker, spouse, child, student) what computer programming is all about. The text can readily be used as a teaching model for anyone playing the role of computer instructor.

Armchair BASIC is dedicated to the proposition that "anyone can learn programming," and is designed for the casually curious as well as for the utterly baffled individual who is finally ready to join the computer revolution. Although other beginning books have been written, this one is for people who haven't bought any of them yet. (It might also be attractive to people who did buy one or more of those other books in an attempt to teach themselves BASIC, but didn't succeed, and want to try again with something new.)

Within the covers of this book you'll find introductory material about computer history, hardware, and software; quizzes that test your recall; and a glossary.

Chapter 1—Computing. From recording the number of mastodons that were felled at the hunt to totaling tax deductible purchases, our species has been obsessed with quantifying aspects of our daily existence. This chapter takes us through a time portal to explore firsthand those moments in history when breakthroughs in computing were made.

Chapter 2—The Equipment. Everything you need to know about the parts of the computer and the instructions that make it work. This chapter talks about the vast, yet hopelessly inefficient, human memory and its computer counterpart.

Chapter 3—PRINT, LIST, RUN, and NEW. The simplest of all BASIC commands are examined from every possible angle. Using **PRINT**, you'll learn how to get the computer to display words and numbers and do elementary arithmetic. The **LIST** command allows you to see what's in the computer's memory, **RUN** executes what's there, and **NEW** erases it.

Chapter 4—Variables. You'll learn about the computer's electronic filing cabinet, how to store information in the computer's memory, and how to get it out again.

Chapter 5—INPUT. Socializing your computer so it becomes interactive is the objective of this chapter. We'll show you how to get the machine to ask questions of innocent passersby and thus hold up its end of a conversation.

Chapter 6—IF/THEN. This chapter deals with setting up the conditions for specific responses in question and answer situations. When the computer can be programmed to selectively respond a certain way, it gives the appearance of actually "listening."

Chapter 7—FOR/NEXT. Now it's time to learn some of the tricks of programming, that is, teaching the machine to do the job using the smallest number of instructions. The **FOR/NEXT** loop is invaluable because it enables the computer to perform a certain task a specific number of times.

Chapter 8—Random Numbers. Playing around with random numbers brings out the gambler in all of us, whether we are guessing what number will be picked, where something will be displayed on the screen, or how many times a flipped coin will turn up heads. Randomizing events with a computer opens vistas of creative programming potential.

Chapter 9—READ/DATA. In this chapter we'll be learning the concept behind the **READ/DATA** command with a program that simulates the role of a telephone directory operator by answering requests for telephone numbers.

Chapter 10—GOSUB. Let a subroutine do all the work for you. Understand subroutines and the world is yours. Here we'll be joining the ranks of highly advanced programmers whose programs often consist solely of dozens of subroutines neatly linked together.

Chapter 11—The Future of Computers. Here is a visit to the future for a look at what might be just around the corner in the three places where most of us spend most of our time.

- At Home—Will it do windows?
- At School—Are teachers an endangered species? Will working with computers turn young minds to mush?
- At Work—Eliminating paper in the office of tomorrow.

Quiz Answers. Answers to quizzes at the end of chapters are found on page 245.

Glossary. The field of computers is fraught with terminology that makes a neophyte feel like he or she just landed on another planet. We define (in plain English) the meaning behind the buzzwords.

This book is for you, dear beginner. We wrote every word of it with the constant recollection of what it is like to be starting out on a quest for knowledge. So relax, read and enjoy, and remember the world of computers belongs to everyone.

Annie Fox
David Fox
August 1982

PROLOGUE

Fred in Technoland

Fred Frantic walked into the computer store with a sense of anticipation mixed with anxiety. The anticipation was, however, most responsible for bringing him to this electronic threshold. That, and his friend and former neighbor Martin, who had been a computer owner and enthusiast for the past four years. It had been very difficult to resist Martin's enthusiastic passion for a device that "makes life easier." And although Fred had successfully resisted it all along, there came a time when his resolve to "not have anything to do with computers" had started to weaken.

When had that happened? Was it when Martin began sending out his Christmas cards with computerized address labels? Or when he stopped commuting 60 miles a day to the office and transferred his whole business to his home? Or was it when he became so successful because of the "instant" access to information for his clients that he was able to buy a beautiful new home for his family (and his computer)? Yeah, that was it. When Martin packed it all in and moved to Plentifield, Fred realized that maybe his resistance to technology had been self-defeating. That's when he decided to visit ChipTown, a local computer retail store.

So there he was. But where exactly was he? It certainly did not look like any store he had ever visited before. It was light and spacious. Uncluttered yet comfortable. Intelligent-looking people were purposefully examining all kinds of impressive and important-looking equipment. Everyone seemed to know what it was all about. He didn't really know what any of it was about, and quite honestly he was uncomfortable and slightly embarrassed. There was a sense of excitement in the room. The whole place reflected the future, and there he was, a sorry throwback from the past. He felt completely out of his element, like the time he had accidentally walked into an Advanced Organic Chemistry Lecture instead of Freshman English.

Fred began having second thoughts about his decision to come. He obviously didn't belong here. He was just about to turn and head for the door,when he spotted a nonthreatening-looking woman with the air of an employee.

"Well, don't just stand here like a dummy," Fred berated himself. "You're here, you might as well find out what's going on." So with a simulated look of assurance, he took a deep breath and a few steps forward.

As he approached, the woman smiled brightly. "Can I help you?" she asked.

"Ummm," Fred stammered, and cleared his throat. "Well, this may sound funny, but I don't really know why I'm here. I don't know the first thing about computers, but my neighbor, actually my former neighbor Martin Miller, has been trying to get me interested in computers for several years. I just haven't gotten around to it until now, and, from the looks of things, maybe I've waited too long. The truth of the matter is, I wouldn't know what to do with a computer if I had one!" Fred blurted it all out and waited for the woman's reaction.

He was pleased to see that she did not seem put off by his total ignorance about computers. She didn't snicker or scoff, but instead thoughtfully inquired, "Would you like to find out a little about what computers can do?"

"Yes," said Fred, feeling better. "I really would."

"Good," said the woman. "By the way, my name is Susan. What's yours?"

"Fred."

"Nice to meet you, Fred. Come right this way."

THE TOUR BEGINS

Susan led Fred over to a chair and a desk that supported a television set perched on top of a flat-looking typewriter.

"This is a microcomputer," Susan began. "It's the kind that you hear referred to as a home or personal computer. It's kind of like a calculator, you know, self-contained. That means it doesn't have to depend on any other bigger and smarter computers to operate."

"Do you call this hardware or software?" asked Fred, figuring it was about time he learned the difference.

"This is hardware," Susan said, rapping lightly on top of the television. "They call it that because it's hard. Software, on the other hand, is just the information that goes inside of the computer."

"Oh, I see," said Fred, brightening. "The hardware is the computer and the software is the stuff that goes inside." Then he paused and, since it seemed safe to appear ignorant, asked, "How does it get in there?"

"One way is through the keyboard. If you know the computer's language, you can just tell it what to do by typing in the information. That's called programming."

"But Martin always said he wasn't a programmer. How did he get the computer to work for him?" wondered Fred out loud.

"He probably bought other people's software, took it home, and popped it into his computer. As long as it was the right kind of software for his computer, the computer would be happy to accept it and go to work."

"I think I understand," Fred said, realizing that it would take a while to actually understand all the details of how the computer did what Susan was describing. Feeling a little bolder, he asked, "Once the information is in there, what can it do?"

"Plenty," Susan said, her eyes getting brighter. "Why don't you have a seat while I show you something?"

Fred was not ready to get too close and said, "I have a knee injury. I think I'd better stand."

With that, she picked up something that looked like a flat black cardboard square with a hole in the middle, and slid it into a box sitting next to the computer. Once the square was completely inside the box, she closed the hatch and pushed a few buttons on the keyboard. A red light on the box went on and Fred heard a whirring noise.

After ten seconds, the whirring stopped, the red light went off, and an animated color picture appeared on the television screen.

"Now this machine has the information it needs to do a special job," Susan said with a marked sense of satisfaction. "We just programmed it with an ecology simulation. As you can see, a growing population of fruitflies is swarming around at the top of the screen. The citrus trees pictured below are being threatened by these hungry critters. Your job is to decide how to handle the pests.

"Well, Fred, the computer is asking you whether you'd like to see your options. Would you like to see them?" she asked.

"I guess so," Fred replied, but he wasn't so sure.

"Well then, go ahead and tell it 'yes.'"

"How do I do that?" Fred was completely mystified.

"Just type in the letter 'y,'" Susan answered.

"You mean you want me to push those buttons?" Fred asked, turning pale. (Suddenly the front door looked very inviting and he wondered whether he had put enough change in the parking meter.)

"Sure, go ahead," Susan encouraged.

"You know," Fred balked, "I was never very good at figuring out these mathematical things."

"There's nothing to it, Fred. It's just like using a regular typewriter. Here's the letter 'y.' Just press it."

Susan made it sound so simple.

"What the heck?" thought Fred, "I'll give it a shot."

Still standing, he placed his finger lightly on the "y," closed his eyes, and pushed.

Much to his amazement, nothing exploded. When it seemed safe enough, he opened his eyes and found that something had indeed happened. The picture on the screen had changed. Where the citrus grove had been, there was now a printed menu of options from which Fred, as manager of the fruitfly eradication program, could select.

After reading all the possibilities, Fred thought that Option Number 3 (heavy and repeated pesticide spraying) would probably be the most effective.

He turned to Susan and asked, "Do I just press a three?"

"If that's the one you want, that's all you have to do," she answered.

He quickly spotted the "3" wedged neatly between the "2" and the "4" and pressed it like a pro, with both eyes wide open.

Once he had indicated his selection, the scene changed again and the computer showed him the consequences of his action. There on the screen he saw birds dropping like rocks from the trees. Small rodents were lying with their feet skyward and the fish in the local stream were swimming belly-up. In addition, because of moderate winds at the time of the pesticide spraying, the pasture adjacent to the citrus grove had inadvertently received a dosage of the pesticide. The dairy cows had ingested the grass and several local milk drinkers had been afflicted with gastrointestinitis.

"Wow," said Fred, totally aghast at the havoc he had wreaked, "look what I did!"

"Don't feel too bad," Susan comforted. "Most people don't do very well, the first time they play this."

"The first time? You mean after the mess I just made, I can get another chance?" Fred was astonished at the forgiving nature of the computer.

"Sure thing," Susan said. "Would you like to try it again?"

"Definitely," Fred answered, sitting down and pulling the chair closer to the computer. "What do I have to press to start it over?"

1 COMPUTING

A history of our need to compute

We had been visiting our local library doing research for this book, when the strangest thing happened. It's not likely that you will believe this, as it was one of those occurrences that doesn't take place very often. We have decided, though, rather than resort to fabrication, that we would submit ourselves to potential ridicule and tell the story as it actually happened.

At the library, one rather hot, sluggish summer day, we asked the reference librarian to help us find some information that would enable us to piece together the history of computing. She was intrigued by the nature of our request, as it seemed that most people who talked to her were children asking her help in finding the answers to questions like "What are the favorite foods of camels and other dromedaries?" Therefore, upon hearing our request and learning that the findings of our research would appear in a book, she was delighted that something of consequence had finally come her way. (We're not sure, but we suspect that some of her initial enthusiasm might also have stemmed from the fact that we promised her an acknowledgment in the book. Her name is Mrs. Vera Klemford, and we thank her heartily for all of her assistance.)

Mrs. Klemford was kind enough to direct us to the Math and Science section of the stacks and promptly left us to our own devices. Eagerly scanning the shelves, we found a book entitled "History of the Number

Seven," one called "The History of Counting Systems Used on Poultry Farms," and one called "The History of Lithuanian Dice Games." While all of these sounded fascinating, they were not exactly what we needed. Downcast and somewhat discouraged, we turned and were about to leave the library, when we noticed a door located to our left and clearly marked "The History of Computing Devices."

The very existence of this door should have struck us as odd, since the library in question is not a large one and we had been there many times without ever having seen it. To tell the truth, though, we were so pleased and excited after seeing the door that we didn't stop to think very much about why we had failed to notice it until now. How fortunate, we thought, that the library is sponsoring an exhibit on the history of computing. And just when we thought our trip here today had been for naught. We might have wondered why the librarian hadn't mentioned it, but, instead, we promptly strode over to the door and opened it.

What we saw inside did not look like any part of any library exhibit we had ever seen. In fact, this room didn't even look like an interior. It was as if we had opened a door and walked right out of the library into some other place. What place it was, we were not really sure. It certainly did not look like the sun-baked streets we had walked along to get to the library that morning. Instead of those familiar streets, we found ourselves walking down a mist covered, dirt path with unfamiliar vegetation on either side. Completely baffled, we walked on for a while, with no idea where we were. Nothing looked familiar, and yet we were strangely compelled to continue.

While we were marveling at the attention to detail and the unerring realism of it all, we suddenly heard some muffled sounds in the distance. As we approached, we saw two ill-shaven, hairy men dressed in animal skins. A small herd of goat-like animals grazed nearby.

From the looks of things, one of the men seemed to be trying to exchange some of his goats for the apple that the other man held in his hand. An apple for a goat? These furry men certainly weren't very bright. We kept our comments at whisper level, but our caution was unnecessary. They were so engrossed in their discussion that they barely noticed us as we stood there.

"How many of your goats will you give me for my apple?" demanded the man with the fruit.

"This many," replied the goatherd, holding up one finger.

The first man looked at the goatherd's finger and grunted. "Not enough," he said.

From the look on his face, the goatherd was somewhat taken aback. Then he held up five fingers and asked, "How about this many?"

"Still not enough," said the man with the fruit. "A man walking with his fat son offered me this many goats from his herd this morning." In saying this he held up ten fingers. "But even that was not enough."

"I will give you more. For that apple I will give you," the goatherd paused and looked down at his fingers. And that's when he realized he had a problem. How could he show more fingers than he had? At that moment he noticed us standing there. And, true to his species, he demonstrated remarkable resourcefulness.

He came over to us and said, "Could you show me where the rain comes from?"

One of us obliged by pointing skyward. At that moment, with fingers outstretched and both arms over his head, he said triumphantly, "I'll give you this many goats!"

The goatherd looked up at all the fingers in the sky and was well pleased. As the man with the fruit nodded his assent, the goatherd thanked us profusely. The goods were exchanged and the two men went off in separate directions and soon disappeared in the mist.

We looked at each other and laughed with appreciation at what we had just witnessed. What a wonderful exhibit, we both agreed. Instead of a display case filled with dusty objects, the library had taken great care to put together this live and extremely vivid representation of how primitive humans used their fingers for computation. Thinking we had seen all there was to see, we turned to find our way back to the door.

The low-lying mist was still rather thick across the path and we were not exactly sure which was the way out. A clicking noise behind us caught our attention and we followed it. Instead of finding a library staff person at a typewriter, as we assumed, we saw a Chinese landowner at the entrance of his granary. Before him stood *hundreds* of men in a long single file. (And we thought the library had to *cut* its budget this year!) The landowner sat on a low stool, wearing silk robes bespeaking prosperity. Beside him was a small writing table with paper and an ink pen. In his lap he held an abacus and his busy fingers were methodically sliding the beads back and forth along several rods.

Remembering our interaction with the goatherd, we now realized that the actors in this exhibit were prepared for audience participation. This in mind, we ventured forth with a question for the landowner.

"What are you doing, sir?" we asked with all the respect due to a man in his position.

He paused in his calculations and signaled the procession to stop. He made a quick notation on his paper, and glanced up at us.

"I am making an inventory of the grain harvest from my many fields. This was a very good harvest as you can see," he said. And with a wave of his hand, he directed us to look at the men lined up at the entrance to the granary. Each one had a full sack of grain thrown across his shoulder.

"This device," he continued, "was brought to me recently. It allows me to tally my grain harvest much faster than was ever before possible. Now, instead of having to rely upon the fingers of many men, or many strokes of the pen, I can slide these small beads on these rods and quickly total the number of sacks that were harvested from each of my fields. This abacus is truly a wonderful device."

After signaling the grain procession to continue, the man held up his hand and stopped them again. Turning to us, he added with a smile, "Now my wife is clamoring for one of her own. She says it will help her determine the number of sweet rice cakes to have the cook make for the children to eat on feast days."

The man bid us farewell and returned to his work in earnest.

We thought how intriguing it was that, even with an abacus, a man could find enough computing to be done to warrant having two such devices in his home.

Enjoying ourselves thoroughly, we wondered, as we walked down the path, just how extensive this exhibit was. Then remembering the sign on the door in the library, it suddenly dawned on us that maybe this was more than just an exhibit. Perhaps, by some fluke, through some unexplainable twist of time and space, we had walked right out of the present into another era, another time.

Before we could take much time to mull over this extraordinary possibility in our minds, an animated young woman wearing a long dress, a shawl, and a bonnet came running toward us.

"Are you two gentlepeople available to see something of scientific note?" she inquired eagerly.

After we replied that we were indeed, she proceeded to tell us the cause for her great excitement.

"My uncle, Charles Babbage, has just completed the first working model of his 'Difference Machine.' He is about to test it out in his laboratory and he has asked me to gather as many interested witnesses as I could find. Would you care to come with me, for what is sure to be an historic event?"

We were delighted once again at our uncanny good fortune—being at the right place at exactly the right time. We happily obliged Babbage's niece and quickly followed her to her uncle's backyard laboratory.

As we were ushered into Babbage's workshop, we joined ten other people, all of them attired in the proper fashion of the English gentry of the early 1800s. Charles Babbage stood proudly next to a 3-foot high mechanical conglomeration of shiny gears and cranks while posing for a sketch. He was a dark-haired man who looked neither old nor young. He had an undeniable look of grim determination about him. Only his bright eyes revealed that his mind was racing off in all directions at once. On the threshold of public triumph, he looked every inch the mathematical genius. The group quieted and Babbage spoke.

"I am delighted to have you all here this afternoon," he began as he put his hand fondly on the machine beside him. "As those of you who know me well will attest, this machine, this Difference Machine, has been a dream—no, an obsession of mine—for the past ten years. And now, on this fair morning in 1822, it is ready for its debut.

"This marvelous melding of gears, wheels, and handles will undoubtedly revolutionize the work of the mathematician. With it I have essentially mechanized addition to such a degree that my Difference Machine can create a table of values for any polynomial. That's right, this small machine can deal with two unknowns in an equation and fully tabulate quadratic functions to the eighth decimal point!"

Although we were not entirely certain what the professor was talking about, and we had our doubts as to the general usefulness of such a machine, it all certainly looked and sounded quite impressive.

"And the common man will also be able to benefit from this invention. I can see it all now. In a year's time these machines will be found on every clerk's desk and in every primary school classroom. Just imagine the drudgery that will be eliminated when each month you can balance your bank account with your own home Difference Machine. What a difference it will make. Why, think of the extra time you'll have for cribbage, cricket, and croquet!

"And it won't be long before you'll see Difference Machineland Shops in Trafalgar Square," Babbage continued. "And then Difference Machine User Groups!"

Well, he had certainly succeeded in getting his group of spectators sufficiently carried away by his vision of a new order. Now for the test that they were all eagerly awaiting.

As a demonstration of the machine's ability, Babbage asked his intelligent niece to create a problem for the machine to solve. When she had done this and had written the answer on a sheet of paper, a gentleman from the audience volunteered to try his hand at solving the same problem. With pen

and paper in hand, Babbage's colleague began working furiously. After Babbage set the numbers and turned the crank a few times, the machine produced the solution. The human completed his work and delivered the same answer a full ten minutes later.

The small crowd cheered in appreciation and Charles Babbage bowed with all the humility a great mind can muster at such times as these.

We exited quietly, not wanting to spoil the party. As visitors from the future, we knew, of course, that poor Charlie Babbage and his Difference Machine were never going to make it big, though he was to be remembered as the "father of the computer."

After wandering away from the scene of Babbage's brief triumph, we saw before us a forbidding-looking building that was marked "C." Upon entering, we were faced with dozens of serious-looking people scurrying about busily. Their dress indicated that we had walked into a more recent era. The central focus of their attention was a massive collection of wires and tubes that filled the entire room.

"May I help you?" asked one woman who was obviously wondering what business two people such as us would have in this place. Her hair was pulled back tightly away from her face, and she wore a 1940s, no-nonsense gray suit complete with shoulder pads. All in all, she was the picture of severity and efficiency.

Sensing that there was some security clearance system in operation here, we cleared our throats and said as nonchalantly as possible, "We're from Building B. We're on a lunch break and have always wondered what was going on in here. What are you guys up to?"

The woman raised an eyebrow and looked us over. Deciding that we didn't look like foreign agents, she relaxed a little and proceeded to tell us about what we had stumbled upon.

"This," she said, waving her arm to encompass the entire room, "is ENIAC." With no small amount of pride in her voice, she continued, "This is the world's first electronic computer. It is the epitome of modern technology. It actually rivals the human brain in some of its capabilities and far surpasses it in others. Do you realize that this machine can perform 5000 mathematical computations in one second? And although it is true that it requires 60 trained technicians working round the clock to operate it, that is but a small price to pay for the computing powers that it offers."

Listening attentively, we began to notice that the room was rather warm.

Our host, who made a point of not introducing herself, began to notice that we were noticing the heat.

"The balmy temperatures you are experiencing are due to the 18,000 vacuum tubes that power ENIAC. Usually we have the air conditioner on to keep things a bit cooler. But we seem to have blown a fuse this morning, and my crew is having a little trouble locating the fuse box. Do you have any questions regarding ENIAC?" she inquired.

We asked what the computer was being used for.

At this, the woman narrowed her eyes and quickly glanced over each shoulder. She took a step closer and lowered her voice. "We are plotting the trajectory of bombs," she whispered. "Even though the war has been over for a year, we still must be prepared. In fact, we are entering the final stages of a very complicated computational process whose results may yield the precise number of air molecules that travel over a conical surface moving at a rate of 180 miles per hour. The computer has been working on this delicate problem for the past 18 hours and we are expecting an answer momentarily."

Just then a young man with an agitated expression ran up to her. But before he could speak our host said, "ENIAC has finally solved the molecular problem! What is the answer?"

The young man, quite red in the face, shook his head. "No answer. This blasted computer just burned out another six vacuum tubes!" Bursting with frustration, he said, "This is the third time this week it's happened. Now we'll have to start the whole calculation process over again!"

The woman received this news without so much as a flicker of a reaction crossing her face. Had it not been for her unusual purple color and the throbbing vein at her temple, we might never have noticed that she was upset. With a tight, quiet voice, she turned to us, forced a smile, and said, "You will have to excuse me. I must attend to a minor malfunction."

Things were getting a little too hot for us there in Building "C," so we decided to leave before our welcome wore any thinner.

On the outside again we noticed that we were on the grounds of a college campus. Judging from the women in bouffant hair styles and cardigans and the beardless men wearing varsity sweaters, we judged ourselves to be in America, around the mid 1960s. Remembering the purpose of this journey, we were pleased, though not at all surprised, to see, right there in front of us, a sleek and modern looking building labeled "Computer Sciences." Having never studied computers in college ourselves, but having made the acquaintance of several doggedly dedicated students who did, we had always wondered what went on in such places. Our recent Building "C" gate crashing still fresh in our minds, we marched up to the door of "Computer Sciences" and, bold as you please, walked in.

We hadn't gone far when we met a young man with the unmistakable look of a computer science major. His eyes were glazed and his clothes disheveled, and he was muttering to himself. And if that wasn't enough to identify him as someone who had just spent the entire night in the programming room, the dead giveaway was this: He was clutching a 3-inch stack of computer punch cards to his bosom.

"Hi there," we said as he walked right by us in total oblivion.

He turned slowly and stared at us. There was a puzzled look on his face as if the sound of a human voice other than his own were strange to him.

"Hello," he finally managed after a few false starts.

"Looks like you've been busy," we said, nodding toward his card stack.

That did it. There's certainly nothing that will draw a programmer into conversation faster than giving him an open invitation to talk about his program.

"I'll say," replied our new friend. "I just pulled an all-nighter punching these cards. We had to write a program that would find the roots of a polynomial using Newton's approximations. I've been working on this one for two weeks, and it's due tomorrow. I sure hope it's right. Everyone taking this Advanced FORTRAN class is really sharp and, to make it worse, the professor used to be a programmer at the Pentagon, and he's an absolute bear. Well, I'm off to feed the cards to the mighty IBM 1130 we've got here and see if it flies. Wish me luck."

He looked back at us to wave goodbye and never even saw the other programmer coming toward him. With her head bent over the page that she was holding and ten feet of computer printout trailing behind her, she was certainly not looking where she was going, but neither was our friend. An instant later they collided, and 321 unnumbered punch cards were strewn across the floor like the wreckage from a gale.

After the impact, he started to scream. And because he kept on screaming, we called for some help from the campus clinic, and two of the medical staff were there within minutes and tried to subdue him. Although our distraught friend was in no mood to listen as they carried him away, we tried to cheer him with the thought that better computing was just around the corner.

Still sympathizing with our frazzled friend, we walked back down the corridor, looking for the way out. Where the front entrance had been, a door marked "Main Library" now stood. We walked right through and, sure enough, we had returned. There we stood, in our hometown library once again. Looking all around to make sure everything was as it had been, we glanced down and noticed an envelope on the floor addressed to us. We looked at each other, picked up the envelope, and opened it. Inside was a single sheet of white paper with the words, "When you need to learn about the future, come back again."

Mrs. Klemford walked by at that moment, saw us, and said, "Did you folks find what you were looking for?"

Hurriedly hiding the note, without really knowing why, we replied, "Yes, thank you, we certainly did."

"Good," she smiled benevolently. "I'm always glad to help."

We left the library in somewhat of a daze. In the car neither of us could talk. When we finally reached home, the first thing we did was race over to our word processor and put down every detail that we could collectively recall. The story is as it stands. You are free to draw your own conclusions. One thing is for sure: Our experiences at the library showed us how much computers have changed.

Today's microcomputers are on their way to revolutionizing society. This entire book is about what you can do with a modern microcomputer. You can learn all about what's current in microcomputer technology starting in Chapter 2. As for the big systems of today, here's the scoop on them.

The CRAY X-MP (made by Cray Research) is one of the most powerful computers around today. It makes ENIAC look like a throwback to the Dark Ages. It is seven feet tall and, occupying 100 square feet of floor space, could fit in a small room. Don't let the compactness of it fool you. This electronic genius can store 288 million characters of information inside of its memory. In terms of speed, it can perform between 100 million and 200 million mathematical operations per second. (ENIAC could only muster a mere 5000 and even then it was always in danger of blowing a tube.) This means the CRAY X-MP could read the name of *every* American in two or three seconds. Sound pretty fantastic? Well, in case you have your heart set on one, you should know that this big, powerful computer is going to set you back about 20 million big ones (dollars, that is).

But it's hard to get too smug about any computer. Like everything else in today's world, computers are changing at a phenomenal rate, and it won't be long before tomorrow's computer applications begin to resemble today's science fiction. Remember, with computer technology, there are no limits beyond those of the human imagination.

You are about to begin a journey of your own.

2 THE EQUIPMENT

Knowing the hardware from the software

Now that we've gained an historic perspective of microcomputers, where do we go from here? To begin with, let's define our terms. A *microcomputer* is an electronic device used to store, retrieve, and manipulate information. It is composed of a keyboard/console and a television-like screen, and is usually small enough to fit comfortably on top of a desk.*

The Brains

Inside the console you will find a *microprocessor,* which is the computer's "brain." This is the place where all the processing of information takes place. The microprocessor is like a film director. It tells the actors (pieces of information) where to go, "decides" what will finally appear on the screen, and oversees the entire production. The microprocessor is really an amazing thing, far less versatile than its human counterpart, but still quite impressive when you think about its size in relation to its power. On the following page, we have a picture of Intel's 8080A microprocessor, greatly enlarged.

---

*Some microcomputers separate the keyboard from the console and house them in separate boxes.

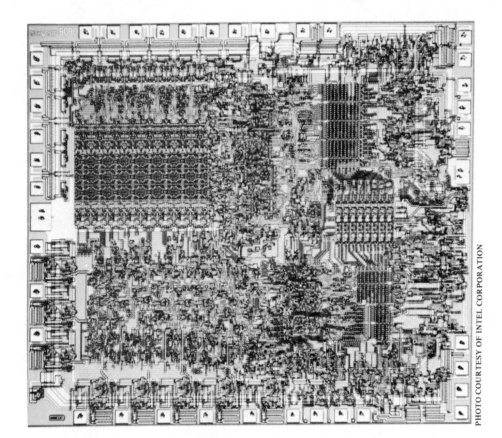

A microprocessor, also known as a *Central Processing Unit* (CPU), is a quarter-inch square of silicon. For those of you who don't remember much from high school chemistry, silicon is the nonmetallic element found in sand. It was really very clever of the researchers who decided to use this to make computer brains. Other than oxygen, silicon is the most abundant element on Earth, and thus it is extremely unlikely that we will ever experience a silicon shortage.

Memory—A Theory

In addition to the microprocessor, the computer also has some other silicon wonders. They are called memory chips and are dedicated to storing information. How much information can be stored depends on how many of these chips the computer has and how many pieces of information they can hold.

The computer, because of the confines of its box and the limitations of current technology, has a rather limited storage capacity. The human, on the other hand, has between its ears a memory which will hold an infinite number of memories. Actually, the distance between two ears is irrelevant since the storage capabilities of the human memory are not a function of physical space (a size 6 7/8 head cannot store more data than a size 6). A computer's memory can be saturated, a human's cannot. And this just goes to show that when it comes to memory size, the human model is superior.

But size notwithstanding, human memory and computer memory are very different. You see, there are two aspects of memory. The first is size (where we definitely come out ahead) and the second is speedy and accurate recall. This is where the computer really puts us to shame because, as you may have noticed, the human memory is not very dependable. Let's look at the reason behind this sad truth.

The human brain (which houses the memory) is a fabulous organ and no one should be without one. The brain controls all of the body's functions, including the recording and processing of sensory input. Whenever you are anywhere with your body, your brain is taking in information through your eyes, ears, nose, tongue, and skin. These sensory data pour in automatically, non-stop all the time, even while you sleep. For example, if you go out to dinner, the information that comprises your "memory" of this occasion is much more complete than your recollection of the color of your friend's shirt or the fact that you ordered filet mignon. While you dine, your brain is receiving information concerning the temperature of the food, the texture of the tablecloth, the smell of the cigar smoke from across the room, and the sound of the unsubtle but plaintive coughs of the cigar smoker's companion.

Although in a week's time you would be hard pressed to remember even what day you went to dinner, all of the details that were recorded at the scene will actually remain in your memory forever. (This has been verified by people who, under hypnosis, have the ability to recall insignificant details of events that took place decades before.) The only problem with this infinite and minutely detailed memory of ours is the total unreliability of the beast. We can't always remember things when we want to, and conversely we often find ourselves dealing with "found" information that we didn't even know we were seeking. First, you can't recall the name of the person to whom you were just introduced, and then a song on the radio triggers a bombardment of scenes from the 1968 senior prom! It's all so unpredictable.

Computer memory is not prone to these frequent and inconvenient digressions. When the computer is given a piece of information to remember, you can depend on the fact that the information will be available to you upon request whenever you come looking for it. It's just a matter of a different kind of filing system. While we tend to continually stuff information into the front hall closet of our minds, the computer fastidiously packs things away in neatly labeled boxes. As roommates, we'd probably be more incompatible than the "Odd Couple."

Bits and Bytes

Information is stored in a computer in small pieces. The smallest piece of storable information is called a *bit,* which is actually an electronic switch that can either be "on" or "off." The computer is based on a series of these electronic switches way down deep inside the microprocessor. Since you can't represent much information with one or two bits, eight of them are grouped together so that the computer can play with them. Beginning programmers rarely come face to face with single bits. They do, however, occasionally deal with these 8-bit packages, which are called *bytes.*

When you talk about how much memory a computer has, the unit of measurement is the byte. So, what is a byte in human terms? The computer uses one byte of memory to store each character you type. For example, the word "computer" takes up eight bytes of memory; that's pretty straightforward. All keyboard characters, including punctuation marks and spaces in between words, use memory space. For example, the address "Cedar Rapids, IA" requires 16 bytes (not counting the quotes).

These days, a bare-bones microcomputer system will come equipped with at least 16,000 bytes (or 16K*) of available storage space. Sounds like a lot? Not really, since we're talking about characters entered from the keyboard and not whole words. The average English word has five characters, plus

---

*Since computer programmers don't like to type extra numbers, the letter K, an abbreviation for kilo, is used for 1000. So 16,000 translates into 16K bytes of memory, sometimes read as 16 kilobytes. Technically speaking, 1K is 1024 and 16K is 16,384 bytes of memory, but that fact is really not significant for the purposes of this book.

one more for a space separating each word. Therefore, a computer that can store 16K bytes is only going to be able to store approximately 2731 words or about five single-spaced, typewritten pages! And after you use up your limit, what then?

ROM and RAM

Before we reveal the answer to that question let's find out a "bit" more about the computer's memory. The computer has two kinds of memory, the first of which is *ROM*, meaning *Read Only Memory*. If ROM were a slate, when the computer is first turned on, the slate would already have a message printed on it. The message is written in indelible ink and protected with plexiglass so that you can't doodle more messages on the board. This ROM slate contains some important information. Usually the place reserved for the computer's essential programs, it probably includes a programming language and, for most microcomputers, that language is BASIC.

The other kind of computer memory is *RAM*. This term stands for *Random Access Memory* and simply means that this is free open space for you to "write" in and "read" from. One way to write on this "slate" is by typing at the computer's keyboard. Unlike the ROM slate, the RAM slate is completely blank when the computer is turned on. It comes with a piece of chalk sitting there ready for you to use. The size of the slate is equal to the number of bytes in your computer's memory. Regardless of the size, though, whenever you feed your computer any information (either the prepackaged kind or some of your own creation), RAM is the place inside the machine where it is all stored.

However, no matter what its size, RAM is not the best place for the long-term storage of information. Unless electricity charges through those little memory chips that make up the writing slate, the chips can't hold onto information. No power, no memory. And so, even if 16K of RAM was enough storage for your purposes, you would still probably want some way to get the information out of RAM and keep it somewhere else. Otherwise you would literally have to keep your computer on day and night. And even if you were willing to do that, you never know when you might be the victim of a power blackout. Or a child might trip over the power cord and disconnect the system! If all of this sounds like an insurmountable problem, never fear; the details have been thought out ahead of time and the solution is surprisingly simple.

SAVING IT OUTSIDE THE COMPUTER

Computer information can be stored or "saved" somewhere besides inside the cramped quarters of the computer. Computer manufacturers have thoughtfully created magnetic memory dumpsters, also known as "external storage media," and they come in several different varieties.

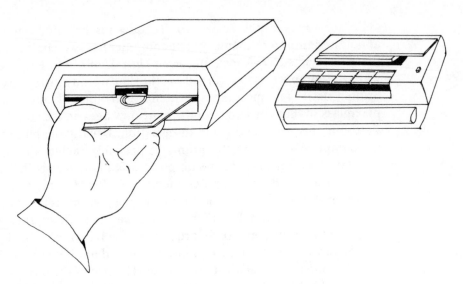

Cassette Tape Storage

The cheapest (and least reliable) magnetic memory dumpster is the cassette tape. Yes, an ordinary audio cassette tape can be used to record and store information from a computer. It is, as you might have guessed, used in conjunction with a cassette tape recorder that plugs directly into the computer. If you have something in the computer's memory which you'd like to save, you simply type in a special command word (which differs depending on the particular machine), and the computer sends the information (in the form of sound) out through the cassette's connection cable and onto the tape.

To get the information from the tape back into the computer to use at a later time, you give the computer a corresponding command, and the information comes back through the cassette cable into the computer's memory again. (By the way, when information is being sent back into the computer, it is *not* being erased from the tape. When you listen to music on a tape, the sound goes into your ear and at the same time stays recorded on the tape. It's the same with digitized computer information recorded on tape. When the information is played back into the computer, the computer is the one with an ear to the recorder.)

Sounds simple? It is, except that cassette storage of information can be exasperatingly slow. It's possible to wait for more than 20 minutes while the information is being saved or retrieved. This is because there is a limit to how much information in the form of sound can be transferred at one time. The transfer rate, called the *baud* rate, will, depending on your computer, range from 300 to 1500 baud, which is the same as 30 to 150 bytes (characters) per second. The larger the section of stored information, the longer it's going to take to make the trip between RAM and the tape. And if the tape was recorded on a tape recorder other than your own, differences in tape speed, volume levels, or alignment of internal mechanisms may result in garbled and therefore unusable information. This is called a "bad load," and if it happens, you have to rewind and try it again.

There's another problem too. To find the information on the tape, you will have to rely on your recorder's tape counter. By making note of tape counter location numbers, you could manually advance or rewind the tape to the correct place. If there is no tape counter on your machine, there could be trouble.

Floppy Diskettes—A Better Solution

These problems don't exist when audio tape is replaced with a different type of storage medium called a *floppy diskette*. The floppy diskette is a cross between a phonograph record and an audio recording tape. It is a flexible, circular disk of magnetically treated Mylar (similar to audio tape) that sits permanently in a square, friction-resistant, protective envelope. The information that is saved on the diskette can be recorded on any available section, rather than in strict sequential order as required with tape.

The diskette, in its envelope, is placed in a *disk drive* (a device analogous to a cassette recorder) and spun around while the *drive head* (analogous to a record player's tone arm) reads information off its surface. Every time the computer places information on the disk, it makes note of the information's location in a "directory," which is also located on the disk. The computer can always find the information again when you request it. The waiting time is negligible (seconds rather than minutes) and nothing is ever misplaced. Although the cost of the disk drive is relatively high ($400 to $1000), this system is undeniably more efficient than any cassette tape recorder.

Suppose you had written a letter on your computer to Ms. Stone. When it's done, you want to clear RAM, that is, empty the computer's memory to give yourself room for a letter to Mr. Green. Not wanting to lose Ms. Stone's letter and not having enough room in the computer for both of them, you store her letter on a disk under the name "Stone" and begin the second letter. When this letter is finished, you store it with the name "Green," turn off the machine, and go to lunch. Because of some pertinent information you receive from a colleague over your tuna salad, you need to make a change in Mr. Green's letter. You want to load it back into the computer and look at it. It's not necessary to know where on the diskette this letter is actually stored. Simply tell the computer to load the "Green" letter and make the change. If you were using a tape recorder instead of a diskette, it could take considerable time before the changes were completed.

Hard Disk Drives—The Cadillac
Of the Storage Medium

If you have lots of information to store and money to spend, you might be interested in the *hard disk system,* the third type of storage media available for microcomputers. The hard disk system uses a rigid platter that looks even more like a phonograph record than a floppy diskette does. This platter is usually permanently sealed in the disk drive cabinet. Compared to the floppy diskette and the cassette tape, the greatest advantage to the hard disk system is that it can store more information (5 to 100 *million* bytes, also called "megabytes," or just "M"). And as for speed, if you thought that floppies were fast, the retrieval time for a hard disk is 4 to 20 times faster! Still another advantage to this system is that several microcomputers can be set up in a network configuration with each of them having access to all of the information stored on the hard disk, that is, the central memory bank.

PUTTING IT ON PAPER

Now that we have examined the way in which the marvelous microcomputer allows us to enter information via a keyboard, view that information

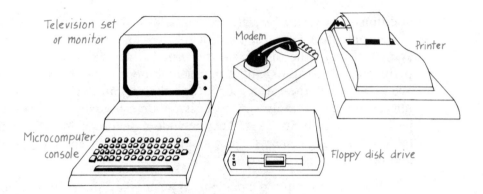

on a screen, and permanently store it on an external storage device, there ought to be a way to put it all on paper. And, indeed, there is. The *printer* is an extremely useful component to any microcomputer system because it enables us to generate a paper copy (sometimes called "hard copy") of any information that is stored inside the computer. The printer can come in very handy when you want to send out letters or reports. A printer can also earn its keep when you want to put information in file folders or carefully examine and edit information from programs whose length exceeds the length of the computer's screen (in which case you would be unable to view all of it at one time).

All kinds of printers are available for microcomputers. Among them are dot matrix printers (which, as their name implies, form their characters from a matrix of tiny dots) and letter quality printers whose copy looks like it has been typed by a human on a fine electric typewriter. The two types of printers are equally reliable and the matrix printer is usually less expensive. Your choice of printers depends partly on the importance of the appearance of the final copy. If you don't care whether your copy looks like it came from a computer, then you can probably do well with a matrix printer. Actually, some of the more expensive matrix printers can turn out copy with a quality that is nearly as good as letter quality printers.

PERIPHERALS—ADDING JUST "ONE" MORE THING

You now know about disk drives and printers, those delightful devices that make your computer an even more valuable tool. And although the addition of these *peripherals* (electronic add-on devices that connect directly to the computer) will certainly provide a computer owner with a complete system of which he or she can be proud, there are other, more exotic peripherals that will expand a microcomputer's capabilities even further. We won't go into these in depth, but you should know they are available for microcomputers at relatively low cost and do enable the small machines to perform in wondrous ways. They include modems, light pens, digitizing tablets, digitizing cameras, voice recognition devices, speech synthesizers, and music synthesizers.

- *Modem* (pronounced moe-dem). A device that connects your computer to your telephone line. This enables you to access the numerous information services that are springing up, or possibly work out of your house. In addition, a modem equips your computer to transfer electronic documents (text) between your computer and any other equipped with a modem. Most of today's modems are directly connected to the telephone wire (called "direct connect"). Others, called "acoustic modems," require you to place your telephone receiver into rubber cups sitting on top of the modem. Direct connect modems are usually more reliable because the sounds of the room will not interfere with your computer's conversations.

- *Light pen.* A pen-like device using a light sensitive transistor that interacts directly with information on the computer screen (CRT). For example, in an educational setting, four objects might be pictured on the screen with the question, "Point to the one which does not belong." To give the computer a response, the student would simply touch the correct picture with the light pen.

- *Digitizing tablet.* A slate-like device accompanied by a special "pen" that enables you to enter graphic information (for example, drawings and graphs) directly into the computer and view it simultaneously on the screen. This can be done without ever touching the keyboard; you just use the pen to "draw" on the tablet. Most of these digitizing tablet systems also come with special features that allow you to draw with different colors and line widths, create circles and squares, and fill large areas of the screen with color.

- *Digitizing cameras.* Essentially video cameras that take the incoming image and break it down into computer-digestible bits. The image can be displayed on the screen, stored on a diskette, and even printed out on paper by a printer.

· *Voice recognition device.* Allows you to "talk" to your computer. When you speak into a microphone connected to this device, the computer does the same thing to your voice that a digitizing camera does with light; that is, it breaks down an audio signal into numeric codes. These codes can then be stored and compared with other codes already being stored in the computer. This is done so the computer can "recognize" the words that you are speaking.

· *Speech synthesizer.* Allows your computer to talk back to you ("Quit pounding on my keyboard" or "If you don't buy me a new printer, I'll tell the IRS the truth about last year's return"). While the light pen and voice recognition device offer computer opportunities to individuals who do not have full use of their fingers for typing, the voice synthesizer can be used by people who are visually impaired.

· *Music synthesizer.* Allows the musician to explore the possibilities of digitized music with more variation than all the stops on an organ. In addition, when a piano-like keyboard is also connected to the computer, a fabulous musical instrument is created. The haunting musical score from the British film, "Chariots of Fire," was composed entirely with a music synthesizer.

SUMMARY

That concludes our hardware chapter. You should be proud of yourself for having learned so much. You now know the difference between RAM and ROM, floppy disks and hard disks, and light pens and ball point pens. You should also have a better idea of how the human mind works, according to one theory. We hope that this brief and informal introduction to the world of computer hardware has put you at ease. You see, it really wasn't as difficult to understand as you anticipated. And just to prove to yourself that you really know what's going on, we've prepared the following little quiz for your enjoyment. Please answer the questions as best as you can and remember to keep your eyes on your own paper. The correct answers to the quiz are found on page 245.

2 QUIZ

1. The computer's brain is made of:
    a. mud
    b. sand
    c. play doh

2. Please complete this analogy. Computer memory is to a filing cabinet as the human memory is to _____.
    a. a skate board
    b. a toaster oven
    c. tangled fishing line

3. RAM means:
    a. Read At Midnight
    b. a male sheep
    c. Random Access Memory

4. The term 24K means:
    a. 240 bytes
    b. 2400 bytes
    c. 24,000 bytes
    d. 24 Karats

5. A popular storage medium is called a flabby disk. True or False?

6. Which of the following is *not* an example of a computer peripheral?
    a. digitizing tablet
    b. disk drive
    c. matrix printer
    d. tennis racquet

3 PRINT, LIST, RUN, NEW

Computer programming: What you would say to a computer if you had the chance

Now that we've given you some fundamental information about the nuts and bolts of the computer, let's get on to the main focus of this book. We are ready to turn from the *hardware* (the metal, glass, plastic, and sand that make up the computer system) to the *software* (the nontangible, internal information for computers). Producing software is the job of *programmers,* those people who write *programs,* which are simply sets of instructions that allow the computer to carry out its tasks.

Starting in this chapter we'll be presenting you with information about how to program a computer, that is, how to write those instructions. This information will be presented in a logical sequence, and each chapter will build on what was covered in the previous chapters. If you find yourself unclear about a concept which was presented, you should really take the time to go over that section again. If you don't, you may find yourself becoming lost in the new material.

Along these same lines, if you have access to a computer, you should definitely take advantage of any and all opportunities to *experiment* with what you've learned. Making actual use of each programming concept does wonders for the learning process. If you don't have access to a computer, you can still reinforce the ideas presented here by trying things out with paper and pencil. Remember, you don't need a computer to write a program (more about this later).

WHAT LANGUAGE DO YOU SPEAK

To give instructions to a computer, you have to be able to speak to it in its own language. What language is that? Well, actually you have your pick of several. Unfortunately, your choices do not include German, French, or even English (though the day when computers have mastered human dialects may not be far down the road). How about choosing either Pascal, FORTH, PILOT, LOGO, or, in our case, BASIC?

BASIC is an acronym for Beginners All-purpose Symbolic Instruction Code. It was developed in 1960 at Dartmouth College by John Kemeny, the father of "Computing for the People." It was originally designed so that students who did not fit the mold of the typical computer science type would have a doorway into what Kemeny considered to be the fascinating world of computers. Thank you, Dr. Kemeny. Your dream of democratizing the study of computers has enabled millions to discover firsthand that these machines are not the heartless, overly ambitious monsters they had been

taught to fear. Instead, they found out that a computer, although extremely "stupid," can be trained as an eager and willing servant.

First Introductions

Let's pretend that we have the pleasure of meeting a visitor from another planet. We know very little about our guest except that it has some linguistic ability. Now the first thing we would want to do in establishing contact with an alien is to make sure it knows we have friendly intentions. After we've established the fact that this particular entity has no functional hearing apparatus, we conclude that perhaps its keyboard-like appendage is the way we can communicate with it.

NOTE: From this point on, all words that are printed in computer type will represent things that appear on the computer's screen. Every line that *we* type into the computer and that appears on our "screen" will be printed in color. Lines the computer has displayed by itself will be printed in black, not in color.

And so we type, tentatively,

```
Hello
```

and the letters instantly appear on the screen, emanating from a small block of light (called the *cursor**). We finish the "o" and wait with bated breath. After a respectful pause, we have the distinct feeling that nothing is going to happen.

While we stare stupidly at the screen, our inner voice tells us that there is some significance to the large button marked **RETURN** (or **ENTER** on some computers) located on the right side of the keyboard. Even though all typing immediately shows up on the screen, the computer cannot receive any information in the place that counts (the brain) until the **RETURN** key is pressed. In other words, *don't forget to hit RETURN*. (This is the most fundamental fact about communicating with computers, so make special note of it.)

---

*The cursor (□) is always found to the right of the last typed character. The place where the cursor appears is where the computer is waiting for you to begin or continue typing. Every computer has a cursor, though it may look like a rectangle, a blinking rectangle, a horizontal line, or a blinking horizontal line.

With some hesitancy we press this special button and something on the screen changes. Underneath the word "Hello" there is a message from the alien. Here it is, world, the first message from a non-earth being. The alien says

```
SYNTAX ERROR
```

What's that supposed to mean? Our inner voice comes to our aid again (it must have taken a programming course without telling us). *Syntax error* means that the computer has no idea what we're saying. The computer is assuming that we made an error in putting together the elements of a BASIC command. Whenever something beyond the realm of its limited understanding is typed into a computer, this brief message or an equivalent one will be displayed. Loosely translated, it means, "I'm terribly sorry. But I simply cannot obey your command because I really do not know what you would like me to do. My sincere apologies for my utter lack of intelligence."

Don't let the word **ERROR** throw your concentration. We didn't really make a mistake in conventional terms. We simply didn't give the computer enough information for it to do our bidding. The computer is as sorry about the whole thing as we are. Let's go ahead and try again. Maybe we can both get it right the next time.

How about something more simple than "Hello"?

```
Hi
```

We try it, and guess what we get when we press **RETURN**? You guessed it, another **ERROR**. What is being displayed here is not just a nonunderstanding of English. Anything from "bonjour" to "shalom" is going to cause the same response, that is, "I don't know what you want!" So now that we've discovered what the computer doesn't know, let's find out what it does know.

PRINT on the Screen

The computer that we're trying to communicate with knows a language called BASIC. Like all languages, BASIC has a vocabulary and a syntax (or sentence structure). Each word is a direct command to the machine. If words are spelled correctly and the syntax is in order, the computer is most willing to work.

The first word we'll learn in BASIC is **PRINT** (not MAMA, PAPA, or IBM). You're right, it looks like English, and that's part of the beauty of it. Because the commands (vocabulary) of BASIC have English equivalents, they are relatively easy for English-speaking people to remember. So let's try out our first BASIC command by typing the next line and see what happens.

```
PRINT "I wonder what kind of creature you are?"
```

When you've finished typing, don't forget to include the quotation marks (") and be sure to press the **RETURN** key. (Always press the **RETURN** key whenever you've finished "saying" something to the computer.)

What happened? Part of what we typed seems to have cloned itself on the screen directly below the original, so that we now have

```
PRINT "I wonder what kind of creature you are?"
I wonder what kind of creature you are?
```

What's happening? Is the computer, in fact, wondering the same thing that we are? Is this some kind of telepathic link? It's doubtful, but let's experiment with something else just to make sure. We type in

```
PRINT "I don't trust computers"
```

and wait to see what our electronic alien will say to that one! (If you're actually doing this at a computer keyboard, don't forget to hit the **RETURN** key when you finish typing. After this, we won't be reminding you every time.)

In a flash the computer responds with

```
I don't trust computers
```

(How about that? It doesn't trust computers either!)

When we type in nonsense characters

```
PRINT "s#D.rvfuA8r,9w>8rv/ndu+fsdf(jsd=jfs"
```

as all of us sometimes do (especially when unsolicited memories cause us to lose our grasp of the current reality of the keyboard), we get in response

```
s#D.rvfuA8r,9w>8rv/ndu+fsdf(jsd=jfs
```

As you can see, *any* character from the keyboard may be enclosed in quotation marks and printed on the screen. (Characters that the computer **PRINT**s out on the screen are called *output*. A line of these characters can be referred to as an *output line*.) Any character, that is, except quotation marks. BASIC does not allow you to enclose quotes within quotes.*

Although we presented the first vocabulary command word in BASIC, we didn't say what it meant. Now it should be obvious that **PRINT** means print! Whenever you tell the computer to **PRINT** something (by following the **PRINT** command with a message enclosed in quotation marks), the computer obliges and prints it on the screen. The message, no matter what its meaning, will always be repeated. If, for example, on a Thursday you commanded your computer to

```
PRINT "Today is Saturday"
```

the computer would respond with the misinformation it was given; in other words, we would get

```
Today is Saturday
```

The computer doesn't know Saturday from Thursday. Its laudable powers of mimicry might give a different impression, but the fact is, *the computer cannot read what is inside the quotation marks*! It is literally an illiterate echo; and if garbage (nonsense, misinformation, and so forth) comes in from the keyboard, then garbage is what will come out on the screen.

---

*You can fake the effect, however, with double *apostrophes* like the ones in the following statement:

```
PRINT "She said, ''How doth the little crocodile?''"
She said, ''How doth the little crocodile?''
```

It Wasn't My Fault, It Was
A "Computer Error"

Aha! Now the truth is out. Nearly all (99.99%) of the gross and fine errors that have been blamed on computers can inevitably be traced to the human who wrote the program (instructions), or the one who had his or her fingers on the keyboard during the process of entering information.

It should be emphasized that the computer is stupid. We're not just being unkind; it really is quite dull-witted. We say this because it has no creativity or reasoning powers of which to speak. It is a literal beast without a speck of imagination. Let's show you what we mean.

If you were to write a letter to your dear mother in Omaha and start off with "Deer Mom," it is unlikely that she would think you had changed your name to Bambi. She would, of course, know what you meant. The computer, on the other hand, is such an imbecile that it never knows what you *mean,* it only knows what you *say.* So if it doesn't do what you say, it's only because you didn't actually say what you meant. Get what we mean? Well, suppose we type the following into the computer:

```
PRENT "I know how to talk to a computer!"
```

Notice how the word **PRINT** was spelled. What response do you think will come from the computer? Don't look now, but it's our old friend

```
SYNTAX ERROR
```

Why? Because **PRENT** is not the same as **PRINT**! And even though your mother wouldn't be thrown by an "e" instead of an "a," if you miss one little byte in a BASIC command, the computer literally cannot understand.

Is that stupid or is that *stupid*? We wonder where all this propaganda about super-intelligent computers comes from anyway? As you can see, it certainly isn't based on reality.

The computer's brain circuits are equally impenetrable if you neglect your quotation marks at the beginning of your message. If we type

```
PRINT Today is my birthday
```

we will get

```
SYNTAX ERROR
```

because we left out both sets of quotation marks. If we type

```
PRINT Today is my birthday"
```

we're also going to get

```
SYNTAX ERROR
```

because we left out the opening quotation marks. (Some computers won't respond with an error message for either of the above cases. What they will **PRINT** on the screen, however, won't be what you wanted.)

But if we type

```
PRINT "Today is my birthday
```

we will get

```
Today is my birthday
```

even though we forgot our closing quotes.

Did the computer finally catch on? Not really. It's just that when you ask the computer to **PRINT** a message, the only hard and fast requirement is that the opening quotes appear at the *beginning* of the text. Omit them at the end, and most computers will let it slide. You will, as we saw above, still get the desired results.

The Personal Calculator

The **PRINT** command can also be used to get the computer to act like a calculator. Since **PRINT** means print, we can tell the computer to print the sum of two numbers by entering

```
PRINT 12 + 12
```

When you press the **RETURN** key after typing that command, you will get

```
24
```

Now wait a minute, you say! How come when we typed our birthday message and neglected the quotation marks altogether we got an error message, and now we've left off the quotation marks on 12 + 12 and the computer doesn't seem to mind at all?

That is an excellent question. We're glad you're paying such close attention to all of this. The answer to why you need quotes around **Today is my birthday** and not around **12 + 12** is simple. **Today is my birthday** is a series of characters strung together and called a *string*. (Until now we have been calling a string a "message.") Letters and punctuation marks enclosed in quotation marks are always strings. Numbers are a different story. Sometimes numbers are part of a message (a street address is a perfect example) and sometimes they are really numbers upon which we want the computer to perform certain mathematical operations. The rule about telling the computer to **PRINT** numbers is this: *If you want to use numbers for a calculation, do not use quotation marks around them!*

You can put quotation marks around a mathematical operation if you want to. For example, you can enter something like

```
PRINT "17 - 6"
```

But if you do, the computer will not do what you expect (that is, if you expect to be able to hit **RETURN** and see the number 11 on the screen, you're going to be disappointed). It's not going to work because when *anything* appears inside quotation marks, the only thing the computer knows how to do is *echo* the material. It doesn't matter if the quoted string is "Let me out of here!" or "1600 Pennsylvania Avenue" or "1 + 1."

Anything that's inside quotation marks is a bona fide string. And if it's a string, then the computer (poor creature) will not be able to differentiate between a number or a letter. When something (whatever it is) is put inside quotation marks, it will be echoed.

Now that this is clear, you won't be surprised to see that when you type

```
PRINT "17 - 6"
```

you get

```
17 - 6
```

Since you know what happens when we put a math problem *inside* of quotation marks and why, let's return to our original problem of 12 + 12.

You should now understand that the computer is going to "read" numbers as *numbers* (and not as characters to be echoed) only when they are presented *without* quotation marks. When you tell the computer to

```
PRINT 12 + 12
```

you are actually saying, "**PRINT** (or display) the sum of these two numbers." When the computer receives a command like this, it will gladly oblige. You see, it's very good at arithmetic and like the obnoxiously smart kid in everyone's eighth grade algebra class, loves to show off. So even though computers, as a species, don't know very much (as we're beginning to see), what they do know, they know very well. Numbers and the absolute logic that governs them are their specialty. Built into BASIC (along with command words like **PRINT**) is an understanding of many mathematical operations, including addition, subtraction, multiplication, division, square root, sine, cosine, and exponents.

Punctuating PRINT with the Semicolon

If you want to have the computer **PRINT** *both* the problem and the answer on one line of the screen, it could be done by entering

```
PRINT "12 + 12 = ";12 + 12
```

In that case, your output line would look like this

```
12 + 12 = 24
```

How come? Well, take a good look at that preceding **PRINT** statement. The first part of it is enclosed in quotation marks. By now we should know that **PRINT** tells the computer to *echo,* which, as you can see by the output line following it, is just what it did. But this time the **PRINT** statement doesn't end with quotation marks, and that's something we haven't seen before. Instead, there's a semicolon (;) up there next to the closing quotes, followed by **12 + 12**, which is *not* enclosed in quotes. We've just seen that the computer can "read" numbers (and thereby treat them as such) only if the numbers remain outside of the quotation marks. Therefore, it shouldn't come as a surprise to see that the unquoted **12 + 12** of the **PRINT** statement resulted in the sum, **24**, in the output line.

What does the semicolon do? In the simplest terms, it acts as a separator, a wall of sorts, which indicates to the computer that even though the quotation marks have closed, "There's more to come on the other side of this fence." Semicolons can be used several times within the same **PRINT** statement if some of the things to be **PRINT**ed are inside the quotes and some of them are outside. Let's take a look at the next example, which uses multiplication (in BASIC, the asterisk [*] is the symbol for multiplication; the symbol for division is a slash [/]).

```
PRINT "We have "; 15 * 6 ;" pencils and "; 6 * 3 ;"pens."
```

This may seem like a jumble of quotation marks and semicolons, but let's examine the statement one section at a time. In this way, we should be able to precisely predict the output line.

The first section, or *element,* of this **PRINT** statement is the string **"We have "**. Since it is properly enclosed in quotes and preceded by a **PRINT** command, the computer will print it as it appears inside the quotes. No surprises there. Next comes a semicolon, which always means "more to come," and the second element, **15 * 6**, which is not enclosed in quotes and thus taken by the computer as a multiplication problem to be solved. This is followed by another semicolon and the third element, **" pencils and "**, a string enclosed in quotes. The fourth element, **6 * 3** (more multiplication), is not enclosed in quotes but has semicolons on either side of it. Finally, the fifth element of this lengthy **PRINT** statement is another string, **" pens."**, complete with its own opening and closing quotes. If you enter this statement into the computer, you'll get

```
We have 90 pencils and 18 pens.
```

As you can see, the semicolons serve another function as well. Not only do they act as separators between elements, but they also have a glue-like property that enables them to connect all the elements together when the output is **PRINT**ed on the screen.

Also note the extra spaces, enclosed in quotes, that follow the words "have" and "and" and precede the words "pencils" and "pens." These spaces are necessary to prevent the answers to the math problems from bumping into the pencils and the pens. If we remove the extra spaces, the output line will look like this.*

```
We have90pencils and18pens.
```

Using semicolons and quotation marks to mix numeric and text elements in a **PRINT** statement is an important BASIC concept. Make sure you understand how it's done before you continue because we'll be working with this same kind of statement again in Chapter 4.

Punctuating PRINT with a Comma

In BASIC, the comma has a function similar to the semicolon. When the comma appears in a **PRINT** statement, it too will have the effect of *connecting* the two elements that it separates. For example, if you enter the **PRINT** statement

```
PRINT "Left","Right"
```

the computer will display

```
Left       Right
```

---

*When **PRINT**ing numbers on some computers, a space before and after the number is automatically printed.

Notice the spaces that appeared between the two elements on the output line. They were put in by the computer as a result of the comma that we typed in. The actual number of spaces will vary, depending on the computer and the length of the element that is being **PRINT**ed. Actually, the computer is not really counting a certain number of spaces. It is really moving to a specified location that has been reserved as the beginning of a new *column* on the screen. In the example above, the "L" is at the beginning of Column Number 1 and the "R" is at the beginning of Column Number 2. Remember, when the computer sees a comma *that is not enclosed in quotes* in a **PRINT** statement, it will automatically insert several horizontal spaces in the output line.

WRITING YOUR FIRST REAL PROGRAMS

Everything we've learned up to this point gives us an idea of what it's like to be at the helm of a computer and give commands. That's great, except for the small fact that none of the commands that we captains have given have been "remembered." If, for example, one of your sailors was lolling around looking for something to do, you might command him to

```
PRINT "Swab the deck!"
```

If you did it this way, you'd only get the deck swabbed for an instant and then the sailor would eagerly appear again with the blankest of faces and wait for another command. The problem is not mutiny; it is simply that the numbskull has not put the command in his memory and stored it there. If you keep saying it the way you've been saying it, you'll never make it stick. Rather than make him walk the plank for insubordination, let's take our electronic sailor in hand and teach him how to remember things.

NEW—The Self Destruct Command

Before we start putting "important" things in the computer's memory, we should first make sure the memory is clear. Memory clearing is done with the BASIC command **NEW** (ah, if it were only that simple to clear out the junk in the garage or the attic). The command **NEW** tells the computer to "Take all the BASIC programming instructions stored in memory and, without pausing a second for deliberation, remorse, or old times' sake, get rid of them!" (all that with one word). In unceremonious terms, NEW means "kill." It is a command that should be used with the utmost caution, because a program that has been killed cannot be "un-killed." In other words, when something in RAM has been NEWed, the only way to bring it back is to re-enter it, line by line by line. (This would not be too much of a problem, of course, if you had saved the program on cassette or disk. See Chapter 2.) So be careful and don't say we didn't warn you.

Let's try it out right now by entering

```
NEW
```

Don't get all excited if the screen doesn't clear. In most cases, it shouldn't. (Clearing the screen is different from clearing the memory, just as erasing the chalkboard does not erase the teacher's mind.) Now we're ready to teach an old sailor a new trick.

Line Numbers—"Making It Stick"

When a number (any number) precedes a BASIC command, that command is received by the computer in a special way. By placing a number *in front of* our PRINT command, the computer's memory will instantly improve. For example, if we say

```
10 PRINT "Swab the deck!"
```

and press RETURN (we know you would have remembered but we just wanted to make sure), you might be surprised to see that *nothing* appears on the screen. Has the computer gone out to lunch? Not likely. It isn't immediately responding to our commands because of the number 10 at the beginning of the line.

This number in front of PRINT is called a line number and can be *any whole number.** (Acceptable line numbers are numbers like 17, 342, or 1100,

---

*Since this is the first numbered line of instruction we are giving to the computer, you might logically wonder why we didn't start with the number 1. The truth is that we could have, but the convention in BASIC programming is to begin with a larger number (like 10 or 100) and proceed to number lines in increments of ten (that is, 10, 20, 30, and so forth). You don't have to do it that way, but if you hold on for a minute, you will soon see that it makes good sense. You should also know that the highest line number that can be used in a program depends on the BASIC being used.

and not like 2.5 or 423 1/2.) It tells the computer that what follows is a command to be stored in its memory. The line number indicates to the machine that it is in a passive/receiving mode, rather than an active/doing mode, and that its job is to swallow the information and sit tight until further notification. All of that is communicated to the computer when you begin a command line with a *number* instead of a *command*.

Giving the Computer Its Instructions

Now we're moving into the major leagues, because we're using the line numbers that all BASIC programs require. A *program* is a set of instructions, each of which is a small step that contributes to the completion of a task. Each of these steps is essential to the task's successful completion and each one must be performed in a particular sequence. The line number at the beginning of each command tells the computer in what order to perform each step. For example, if we created a program for an automated kitchen to make eggplant parmesan (written in BACIC, Bakers All-purpose Culinary Instruction Code), the steps might look something like this.

```
 10 WASH eggplant with cold water
 20 SLICE eggplant in paper thin slices
 30 SLICE mozzarella cheese
 40 COVER bottom of baking dish with sauce
 50 ADD enough eggplant slices to cover sauce
 60 PLACE a cheese slice on each eggplant slice
 70 COVER eggplant and cheese with sauce
 80 PLACE enough eggplant slices to cover sauce
 90 PLACE enough cheese slices to cover the eggplant
100 POUR enough sauce to cover everything
110 SPRINKLE parmesan cheese on top
120 BAKE at 350 degrees for 45 minutes
```

As you can see, a program is just a series of steps, the execution of which gives a certain end result. A program may be designed to calculate the number of air molecules passing over a jet's right wing or print "I love you" in the middle of the screen. The computer never makes value judgments, and it will certainly never refuse to execute a program because the task to be done is just too ridiculous. We mention this so you won't feel the need to dream up "important" programs right off the bat. Getting used to writing programs takes some time, and it's perfectly acceptable to indulge in a bit of whimsy while you're mastering the rules (it's also okay to be whimsical *after* you've mastered them).

Now that we understand what a program is, we should tell you that typing the eggplant program into your computer won't get you much of anything. The computer, unfortunately, does not understand commands like **WASH**, **SPRINKLE**, and **BAKE** (though if you go into your kitchen and execute the program yourself you will end up with a delicious meal). If you are going to write a program for a computer, you first have to make sure you're commanding it in a language that it understands. Although we can't get the computer to actually make eggplant parmesan for us, we can get it to remember the recipe and display it on the screen. Here's what that program would look like.

```
 10 PRINT "RECIPE FOR EGGPLANT PARMESAN DELUXE"
 20 PRINT
 30 PRINT "WASH eggplant with cold water"
 40 PRINT "SLICE eggplant in paper thin slices"
 50 PRINT "SLICE mozzarella cheese"
 60 PRINT "COVER bottom of baking dish with sauce"
 70 PRINT "ADD enough eggplant slices to cover sauce"
 80 PRINT "PLACE a cheese slice on each eggplant slice"
 90 PRINT "COVER eggplant and cheese with sauce
100 PRINT "PLACE enough eggplant slices to cover the
    sauce"
110 PRINT "PLACE enough cheese slices to cover the
    eggplant"
120 PRINT "POUR enough sauce to cover everything"
130 PRINT "SPRINKLE parmesan cheese on top"
140 PRINT "BAKE at 350 degrees for 45 minutes"
```

Lines 10 to 140 are called a program *listing*. They are all the instructions that we have given to the computer and that are being stored in its memory. Looking at the entire program now, do you understand each line? With the exception of Line 20, it should all look familiar. Line 20 tells the computer to **PRINT** a blank line. When the computer executes Line 20, its output will be a blank line that will visually separate the title from the rest of the recipe. In this case, since we really don't want the computer to echo anything, quotation marks for this **PRINT** statement are not required.

RUN—All Right, Now Do It

Even though we have written a *series* of commands for the computer to execute, the way in which it executes them is not really any different from the way in which it executes the series when the line numbers aren't there. Except for one important thing. When a line number precedes a command, the computer will *not* execute it instantly. When line numbers are present, the computer's job is to swallow the information and sit tight until it gets the go-ahead signal. The computer can be signaled to switch from the receiving mode to the "do it" mode with a special command called **RUN**.

One last thing before we flip this "switch." Whenever you look at a program, you should be able to interpret it. Knowing what the **PRINT** command means to the computer, you should be able to look over each line and know what will happen when the computer starts to work.

Now that the program is written and your understanding of it is complete, we are ready to see if it works. As we have seen, we have to do more than simply type in the numbered lines of instruction. If we type in lines 10 to 140, the computer will take each one and store it, in sequence, in its memory. Storing information and using it is similar to recalling the process of riding a bicycle and actually getting on the bike and riding. The computer now has all the information it needs to execute this program. It is time to ride.

To send the computer on its way, the programmer (that's you, kid) types the word **RUN** (without a line number preceding it and without the **PRINT** command and without quotation marks), presses the **RETURN** key, and watches the sentences of the recipe appear on the screen as shown at the top of the next page.

There you have it! Now, if you're wondering whether the computer still has your program safely stored in memory, type **RUN** again. In fact, type **RUN** three or four times (making sure you press **RETURN** after each time). Every time you tell the computer to **RUN** the program, it does and the screen is now overflowing with our eggplant recipe. With this three-letter word, the computer will repeatedly and tirelessly carry out all the commands of your program. **RUN**! What a sense of power this gives!

```
RUN

RECIPE FOR EGGPLANT PARMESAN DELUXE

WASH eggplant with cold water
SLICE eggplant in paper thin slices
SLICE mozzarella cheese
COVER bottom of baking dish with sauce
ADD enough eggplant slices to cover sauce
PLACE a cheese slice on each eggplant slice
COVER eggplant and cheese with sauce
PLACE enough eggplant slices to cover sauce
PLACE enough cheese slices to cover eggplant
POUR enough sauce to cover everything
SPRINKLE parmesan cheese on top
BAKE at 350 degrees for 45 minutes
```

LIST—Putting the Script On the Screen

We have been putting information in the computer (with line numbers and **PRINT** commands) and watching our commands being executed on the screen with **RUN**. It has all been working beautifully. Now suppose you wanted to take a look at that listing of original instructions again to make sure everything is still intact. This can be done easily with the BASIC command **LIST**.

In plain English, which is always the best kind, **LIST** means, "Take the complete BASIC program that you are storing in your memory and display (put) it on the screen so I can take a good look at it." Since every command with a line number is being placed in storage, it is very useful for the programmer to be able to see what's in there so that changes, additions, and deletions can be made. Because **LIST**, like **RUN**, is not a command to be stored in the computer's memory, but rather to be acted upon directly, it is called a *direct mode* command and *never* requires a line number. Remember that.

We give it a whirl and get

```
LIST

10 PRINT "RECIPE FOR EGGPLANT PARMESAN DELUXE"
20 PRINT
30 PRINT "WASH eggplant with cold water"
40 PRINT "SLICE eggplant in paper thin slices"
50 PRINT "SLICE mozzarella cheese"
60 PRINT "COVER bottom of baking dish with sauce"
70 PRINT "ADD enough eggplant slices to cover sauce"
80 PRINT "PLACE a cheese slice on each eggplant slice"
90 PRINT "COVER eggplant and cheese with sauce"
100 PRINT "PLACE enough eggplant slices to cover sauce"
110 PRINT "PLACE enough cheese slices to cover the
     eggplant"
120 PRINT "POUR enough sauce to cover everything"
130 PRINT "SPRINKLE parmesan cheese on top"
140 PRINT "BAKE at 350 degrees for 45 minutes"
```

If you're thinking that the execution of the program (the **RUN**) looks suspiciously like the program itself (the **LIST**), you're right, sort of. The sentences are the same, but in the listing of the program there are line numbers, **PRINT** commands, and quotation marks, all of which are missing when the program is **RUN**. This makes perfect sense if you remember that when we told the computer to

```
PRINT "Today is my birthday"
```
we got

```
Today is my birthday
```
without **PRINT** and the quotation marks.

In other words, on the stage of Digital Drama, the computer is the actor, and the playwright is the programmer. The listing contains the lines the computer is given to learn. The performance will only take place when the playwright/director gives the action command (**RUN**). The **LIST** command will only provide the playwright with a copy of his or her play.

Semicolons, Gluing Two Lines Together

As we mentioned earlier, the semicolon is used in a **PRINT** statement to connect elements. If used at the end of a **PRINT** statement, the semicolon can also connect that statement to the next **PRINT** statement, as demonstrated in the following lines:

```
NEW

10 PRINT "You never can tell when you might need a ";
20 PRINT "piece of tape."
```

These are two separate **PRINT** statements on two separate lines. Yet because of the semicolon hanging on the end of Line 10, when the program is **RUN** the following output appears:

```
RUN

You never can tell when you might need a piece of tape.
```

Although you might not be able to imagine any practical application for this property of semicolons, it will come in handy in a later chapter. Just remember that you heard it here first.

Adding Additional Lines

There are a few more things to know about line numbers. As we mentioned earlier, line numbers can be any whole number, and even though we began our program with Line 10, that is not a requirement. It is permissible to begin numbering your lines with the number 100 or 4 or even 1 (if you are the type who doesn't like to stray too far from the norm). Actually, it doesn't matter at all what number you begin with, but it does make good sense to skip some numbers between each new number and the previous one. Here's why.

Writing a program in BASIC could be compared to a leisurely amble through the woods. You know what your eventual destination will be, but you're not really in a hurry. During the walk you often stumble across things that make your journey more enjoyable. BASIC provides the freedom to create as you go along, and since the computer will accept your numbered commands in whatever order they are typed, it's possible (although not necessarily advisable) to write a program without planning ahead.

Some people think that this freedom is just great because ideas can flow unencumbered by any rigid structure. On the other hand, those who program in languages like Pascal (which encourages a program to be precisely thought out ahead of time) deplore the "shot in the dark" manner often associated with BASIC programming. In truth, if you ever tackle a large programming project, the "come what may" approach will probably backfire; you may get lost in the forest of your program. But for now, just enjoy the trees.

As you write numbered instructions for the computer, it is often the case that as an afterthought you will want to go back and "stick in" another thing or two. If you were numbering your lines in a 1-2-3 sequence, and then decided to add something between lines 2 and 3, there would be a problem since a line number can only be a *whole* number. (Where have we heard that before?) By numbering the same three lines of instructions with a 10, 20, and a 30, however, there would be no difficulty in squeezing another line (or another nine lines) between 20 and 30. Here's what we mean. Let's clear the memory and begin with something new.

```
NEW
```

Suppose our new program looked like this.

```
10 PRINT "Once upon a time there was a frog."
20 PRINT "He loved to sit and catch flies."
30 PRINT "Then a fly who would not be caught flew by."
```

That looks pretty good. Now, if we want to add a line between 20 and 30, how do we do it? First, pick a number between 20 and 30; any number will do. Let's use 25. Then we'll type in the line we want to add (making sure it's preceded by the line number, 25), like this:

```
10 PRINT "Once upon a time there was a frog."
20 PRINT "He loved to sit and catch flies."
30 PRINT "Then a fly who would not be caught flew by."
25 PRINT "He was the best fly catcher in the outfield."
```

If it looks a bit out of sync, don't worry! As we said before, the computer is just a whiz when it comes to anything having to do with numbers. Our electronic friend *knows* that 25 does not come *after* 30. Let's **LIST** this program and watch how the computer puts everything in its proper place.

```
LIST

10 PRINT "Once upon a time there was a frog."
20 PRINT "He loved to sit and catch flies."
25 PRINT "He was the best fly catcher in the outfield."
30 PRINT "Then a fly who would not be caught flew by."
```

There you have it. Notice how the computer put our Line 25 right where it's supposed to be? (And you were worried!) Now, when you **RUN** this program, even though the lines were entered out of numeric sequence, the computer will **PRINT** it out like this.

```
RUN

Once upon a time there was a frog.
He loved to sit and catch flies.
He was the best fly catcher in the outfield.
Then a fly who would not be caught flew by.
```

As we just saw, the order in which the commands are typed is not significant. A command's line number is the only thing that determines its position in the execution (**RUN**) sequence.

Making Some Changes

As we entered (typed) our little amphibian program, it was stored in the computer's memory. Suppose after **RUN**ning the program (as we did previously) we wanted to make a change. The first thing we'd do is **LIST** it. (You don't really have to **LIST** a program before changing a line, but it is a useful thing to do, in case you've forgotten the number of the line you want to change.) When we do that, we get

```
LIST

10 PRINT "Once upon a time there was a frog."
20 PRINT "He loved to sit and catch flies."
25 PRINT "He was the best fly catcher in the outfield."
30 PRINT "Then a fly who would not be caught flew by."
```

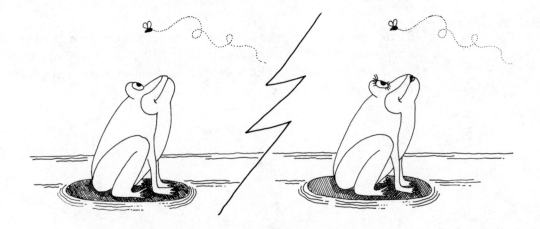

Now that we've seen it, we can go to work. Just so we don't ignore all those

great female outfielders, let's do a little editing. To make a change, first identify the number of the line to be changed. The list shows that the first change needs to take place on Line 20, where the text should read "She" instead of "He." The most fundamental way of changing something on a computer, guaranteed to work on *any* machine, is to *enter the corrected line using the same line number.* Enter a new Line 20, and when you've finished, the screen should look like this.

```
LIST

10 PRINT "Once upon a time there was a frog."
20 PRINT "He loved to sit and catch flies."
25 PRINT "He was the best fly catcher in the outfield."
30 PRINT "Then a fly who would not be caught flew by."
20 PRINT "She loved to sit and catch flies."
```

At this point, it looks like there are two Line 20s on the screen (which, in fact, there are). But two Line 20s are not being stored in the computer's memory, and that's where it counts. You say you're not so sure about that? Well, we have a sure-fire way to prove it. Remember the **LIST** command we just told you about? It means, "Display on the screen the list of BASIC instructions which is now in memory." So if we were to **LIST** this program right now, we should be able to see which Line 20 the computer is holding onto. Here is the current listing for all to see.

```
LIST

10 PRINT "Once upon a time there was a frog."
20 PRINT "She loved to sit and catch flies."
25 PRINT "He was the best fly catcher in the outfield."
30 PRINT "Then a fly who would not be caught flew by."
```

Pretty tricky, but what happened to the original Line 20? We'll tell you (remember, we're here to reveal all the tricks of the trade). The computer can only store one line for each line number. When we entered a new Line 20, we displaced the old Line 20 (a fancy way of saying "threw it out"). You can keep changing the "he" to "she" and "she" to "he" as many times as you like, but when you **RUN** or **LIST** the program, the change that will remain is the one that was last entered. While we're at it, let's fix Line 25 in the same way. When we **LIST** and enter the new Line 25, we get

```
LIST

10 PRINT "Once upon a time there was a frog."
20 PRINT "She loved to sit and catch flies."
25 PRINT "He was the best fly catcher in the outfield."
30 PRINT "Then a fly who would not be caught flew by."
25 PRINT "She was the best fly catcher in the outfield."
```

Then **LIST** the program one more time (just to make sure the computer is doing its job) and the following sequence appears:

```
LIST

10 PRINT "Once upon a time there was a frog."
20 PRINT "She loved to sit and catch flies."
25 PRINT "She was the best fly catcher in the outfield."
30 PRINT "Then a fly who would not be caught flew by."
```

The new Line 25 is in place, and everything looks fine. Now **RUN** the program and the screen displays

```
RUN

Once upon a time there was a frog.
She loved to sit and catch flies.
She was the best fly catcher in the outfield.
Then a fly who would not be caught flew by.
```

So far so good. You know how to add and change lines in a program. Now there's one more thing you need to know before we close the chapter and give you a breather, and that's how to delete a line from a program entirely.

Deleting a Line

If a line in a program is beyond the point of being correctable (if, by some chance, you *really* made a mess) or if a line is no longer needed or wanted, the best thing to do is get rid of it. The method used for deleting a line is similar to the one used for changing a line. To delete a line, simply enter the number of the line you'd like to delete and press **RETURN**. Entering a line number with nothing after it *replaces* the existing line with nothing, in other words, deletes the existing line.

All this talk about deleting lines has made us wonder about whether we really want to keep that line about the fly that wouldn't be caught. It is a bit of a cliff-hanger and may not be appropriate for the last line of a story. Let's delete it. The process, which we've just outlined, is simple. First we'll **LIST** the program.

```
LIST

10 PRINT "Once upon a time there was a frog."
20 PRINT "She loved to sit and catch flies."
25 PRINT "She was the best fly catcher in the outfield."
30 PRINT "Then a fly who would not be caught flew by."
```

Now we'll type 30 and hit **RETURN**.

```
30
```

Then, just to make sure that the magic works, let's **LIST** it again and see what we have left.

```
LIST

10 PRINT "Once upon a time there was a frog."
20 PRINT "She loved to sit and catch flies."
25 PRINT "She was the best fly catcher in the outfield."
```

Voilà! The offending Line 30 has been forever stricken from memory.

Now that we've got our script in perfect order, we're ready for the performance. We'll just tell the computer to **RUN** while we sit back and enjoy our little story.

```
RUN

Once upon a time there was a frog.
She loved to sit and catch flies.
She was the best fly catcher in the outfield.
```

That's it. Not bad for a beginner. Since this lesson is just about over and we aren't interested in holding onto the frog program, let's tidy things up by clearing the computer's memory.

```
NEW
```

In case you're wondering what would happen if you tried to **LIST** the program now, here it is.

```
LIST
```

What happened to the program? We NEWed it, and that really *does* erase everything in the computer's memory; therefore, there's nothing left to LIST.

Congratulations! You did it! You wrote a program, LISTed it, ran it, added a few lines, made a change here and a deletion there, LISTed it, and ran it again. Then when you were done you threw it all away. Go get yourself some milk and cookies, and relax a little. The end of chapter quiz is starting in five minutes.

SUMMARY

Giving commands to the computer can be a real confidence builder, as we saw in this chapter. By learning some simple statements in the electronic alien's language we managed to communicate with it. Always remember that **PRINT** means print, **RUN** means execute, **LIST** means list, and **NEW** means kill or erase. Now with all this information fresh in your mind, you're ready for the quiz.

3 QUIZ

1. The most popular programming language for microcomputers is:
   a. FOIBLE
   b. THIRD
   c. PLASTIC
   d. BASIC

2. If you enter:

   ```
   PRINT "Wednesday is Friday the 13th"
   ```

   the computer will respond with:
   a. Wednesday is Friday the 13th
   b. SYNTAX ERROR
   c. "Wednesday is Friday the 13th"
   d. Sorry, Wednesday is the 11th

3. True or False: When you want the computer to perform a mathematical operation, make sure you enclose the problem in quotation marks.

4. To clear the BASIC program from the computer's memory, the command is:
   a. OUT, OUT!
   b. KNEW
   c. NEW
   d. Will you please leave?

5. If you want the computer to remember a command, you must always precede that command with a:
   - *a.* telephone number
   - *b.* line number
   - *c.* credit card number
   - *d.* please

6. To squeeze a new program line between lines 40 and 45, you should:
   - *a.* begin the new line with 42.5
   - *b.* begin the new line with any whole number from 41 to 44
   - *c.* start over, it's no use
   - *d.* use a shoehorn

7. A mistake on Line 15 can be corrected by:
   - *a.* turning the computer off
   - *b.* using a memory chip eraser
   - *c.* entering a new Line 15
   - *d.* sincerely apologizing for your *faux pas* and asking the computer if it would mind fixing it for you

8. The best way to delete Line 40 from a program is by typing:
   - *a.* **NEW**
   - *b.* **LIST**
   - *c.* **RUN**
   - *d.* 40
   - *e.* all of the above

9. The computer displays all information in its memory when you type:
   - *a.* **LIST**
   - *b.* **LUST**
   - *c.* **LOST**
   - *d.* Show Me My Program!

10. Generally speaking, computers are:
    - *a.* philanthropic
    - *b.* sentimental
    - *c.* obstinate
    - *d.* none of the above

4 VARIABLES

Storing your blues away in little memory boxes

Now that we know how to get the computer to display information on the screen (using the **PRINT** command), we are ready for the next step. This involves putting specific pieces of information (data) in special boxes and storing them in the computer's memory so they can be dredged up at will. Being able to store information electronically is a feature unique to computers and, as we mentioned in Chapter 2, one that we humans find extremely beneficial.

THE STORAGE BOX

A computer storage box is called a *variable,* from the Latin word *variare,* meaning "change." The name is appropriate since a variable's contents can be *changed.* We recall being introduced to the term in Elementary Algebra class where it was invariably associated with X's, Y's, and Z's. In deference to those of you with unpleasant memories of a similar time in your lives, we promise that you will never find a variable called X, Y, or Z in this book!

Naming the Boxes

Suppose you have holiday decorations stored in boxes in your attic or garage. Each box is sealed, is identical in shape, size, and color, and totally lacks any external identification. The only way to locate the Thanksgiving decorations is to open each box until you find the right one. This could be quite a job, one that would be completely unnecessary if the outside of each box bore a label of sorts. (Many people dislike this degree of organization, as it prevents them from storing things wherever they want.)

The use of variable boxes inside of the computer is similar to what's going on in the attic. There are two main differences, however. First, since the computer abhors confusion, BASIC requires that a variable be labeled as soon as you begin using it; no one, on the other hand, is standing in your attic with a label maker and a whip. Second, BASIC has *two* types of variables to hold two very different kinds of information, but a cardboard box can hold anything.

The first type of variable can hold *any* series of characters you desire. Because these characters are *strung* together like beads on a necklace, they have been named *string variables*. String variables are great for holding names of people, poetic phrases, different flavors of jam, street addresses, and the like.

However, there is one thing you can't do with the contents of string variables, and that is math. (The computer won't let you add "strawberry jam" and "orange marmalade," even though it might create a wonderful new flavor.) If you do need to add two things, you're going to have to do it with the second type of computer storage box, *numeric variables.*

Numeric variables are *only* used to store *positive or negative numbers,* which can then be added, subtracted, squared, and so on. That sounds like a straightforward statement, but be aware of the fact that not everything containing a number can be put into a numeric variable. The following are examples of numeric values that *can* go into a numeric variable:

```
17      12.725      104234      0      -35
```

Numeric values that *cannot* be put in a numeric variable include such examples as

```
6,432      $1.43      (213)555-1212
```

They won't work because in addition to numbers they contain commas, dollar signs, and parentheses—all of which are nonnumeric characters.*

Since the two kinds of variable boxes look identical from the outside, the computer needs something with which to distinguish them. Therefore, the *name* of every variable tells the computer which *kind* of box it is (string or numeric).

If the variable is a string variable, the last character in the name is a *dollar sign.* The dollar sign (**$**) *always* tells the computer that you mean string variable. To help you remember this, think of the dollar sign (**$**), which looks like the letter "S," as standing for String. All of the examples that follow can be used as names for string variables:

```
FOOD$      N3$      ANIMAL$      CAR$      ADDRESS$
```

They work as string variables because the final character in each is a dollar sign (**$**).

Without a dollar sign in the variable name, the computer assumes that you mean numeric variable. All of the following are viable names for numeric variables:

```
A2      AREA      NUMBER      WEIGHT      AMOUNT
```

Because the final character in each name is a letter or a number (but *not* a

---

*Placing a phone number such as 555-1234 into a numeric variable will cause the computer to perform the subtraction 555 *minus* 1234. The number actually stored would then be – 679!

dollar sign) these examples can function as numeric variables.

The choice of a variable name can be an arbitrary one. A variable name can be any single letter or a combination of letters and numbers. (Depending on the computer, however, there may be restrictions on the number of characters you can use in the name or on the actual choice of name.)

The actual name you choose, however arbitrary it may be, should have some association with the variable's contents. Naming variables by association makes it easy to remember which variable box is storing what. In other words, you *could* label the box of Thanksgiving decorations "bananas" if you wanted to, but we certainly wouldn't recommend it.

The general rules for naming variables that apply to all computers are

- A variable name must be at least one character long (in addition to the dollar sign). For example, A could be a variable and so could A$, but $ could not.

- In most BASICs, the letters of a variable name must be entered in upper case (capitals).

- The first character of the variable name must be a letter of the alphabet, but the characters that follow may be letters or numbers. In other words, you could call WEIGHT2 a variable but not 2WEIGHT.

- If you are naming a string variable, the name must end with a dollar sign symbol ($). By this we mean that CITY$ is a string variable and CITY is not.

- If the name represents a numeric variable, a dollar sign is not used. Therefore, CASH$ cannot be a numeric variable, but CASH can.

All BASICs are Basically the Same

It's true that all the dialects of BASIC are basically the same, but every now and then you will come across some differences. Here's one of them. In some dialects of BASIC, only the first two characters of a variable name are noticed by the computer.

A variable called JOB, for example, might be considered by the computer to be the same as a variable called JOHN since the first two characters of each name are JO. (To discover the specific requirements for naming variables, it is advisable to check the BASIC manual that comes with your computer.)

Reserved Words—You Can Call It Almost Anything

One other important aspect of naming variables is a knowledge of which names are absolutely off limits. Because variable names are never enclosed in quotation marks, the computer really does read them. Therefore, they must not be the same as any BASIC command word.

Command words are reserved exclusively for other purposes. (They are, in fact, called *reserved words*.) For example, you could not legally call a variable **RUN** or **RUN$**. The same is true about using **LIST**, **PRINT**, or **NEW**. As a matter of fact, in some BASICs you are also restricted from using a variable name that has some reserved word *embedded* (included) within it. For example, **CRUNCH**, **GLISTEN$**, and **SPRINT** are all no no's because they contain the reserved words **RUN**, **LIST**, and **PRINT**, respectively.

For the BASIC commands that you know, there won't be too much of a problem remembering what to avoid. As for BASIC commands that you don't know, you could get into trouble without being aware of it. If the computer keeps giving you a syntax error on a statement that appears to be perfect, then you might be trying to use a variable name containing a reserved word. Just to make sure, try altering the variable name to something else and see if the computer likes the line any better.

Make sure you check your BASIC manual for a complete listing of reserved words and avoid them as variable names. The truth is, receiving an **ERROR** message is the worst thing that can ever happen if you do something "wrong" on a computer.

Unlike the chemistry lab, where experimentation is fraught with danger, there are really no negative consequences to computer experimentation. In fact, you should use the computer's compulsion to inform you of mistakes as a learning tool. The instant feedback it gives you can be the best teaching aid around for learning BASIC!

FILLING THE BOXES USING LET

Now that we know what's legal when it comes to christening a variable, let's see how we go about storing something inside.

Using String Variables

Whenever you wish to put some data into a variable, you can use a special BASIC command called **LET**.* This data can be numbers, words, or a combination of the two (depending on the type of variable). For example,

```
NEW

10 LET NAME$ = "Macbeth"
```

This single line provides the computer with much important information. The number 10, of course, is a line number. It tells the computer that what follows is a command to be stored in memory and kept there until further notification. In our example, Line 10 means, "Create a string variable, call it **NAME$**, and store the string of characters *Macbeth* inside of it." In more important sounding terms, what we've just done is "assign a value," *Macbeth,* to the string variable **NAME$**.

Notice that the last character of our variable is a dollar sign ($)—that's how the computer knows **NAME$** is a string variable. Notice also that Macbeth is enclosed in quotation marks. Don't let the quotation marks here confuse you. This is a **LET** statement, not a **PRINT** statement.

The quotation marks tell the computer that the enclosed string of characters is the thing that will be put inside the variable. It may seem like just another detail to you, but these quotation marks are definitely *not* optional. If you leave them off, you're going to get a syntax error.

If you impatiently raced ahead and ran this program, you shouldn't have been too surprised when the computer displayed nothing. Without a **PRINT** statement, a program that is **RUN** will not display anything. That being the case, we ought to add

```
20 PRINT NAME$
```

Before you go ahead and **RUN** the program to see what happens now,

---

*The use of the word **LET** is actually optional in most BASICs. Writing 10 NAME$ = "Macbeth" would work just as well as 10 LET NAME$ = "Macbeth". The use of **LET**, however, makes the program more readable, so we will always use it throughout this book.

please notice that even though we are using the **PRINT** command and *not* using numbers for a calculation, we have no quotation marks around **NAME$**! Although this seems to be in direct contradiction to what we told you in Chapter 3, if you think about it carefully it *will* make sense.

DIM—Using String Variables in Atypical BASICs

If you have access to a computer that is not using a version of Microsoft BASIC (for example, ATARI standard BASIC), a preceding step must be added before you can use string variables. For every string variable in your program, you need to reserve memory space for it by telling the computer the *maximum length* (in characters) of the string you want to use.

This is done with a **DIM** (for **DIM**ension) statement, which always precedes the first occurrence of the variable. The use of this statement is similar to making a reservation at a motel before you check in. For example,

```
5 DIM NAME$(25)
```

tells the computer that the variable **NAME$** will have a maximum length of 25 characters.

If you have several string variables to **DIM**, you can put them all on the same line and separate them with commas. For example, you may enter

```
5 DIM NAME$(25),SPOUSE$(33),VERB$(15)
```

A variable may only be **DIM**ensioned *once* in a program. Trying to re**DIM**ension it by sending the computer back to the **DIM** command will result in an error message.

Note that a **DIM** statement is used in versions of Microsoft BASIC, but in those versions it has a different use, one that we will not be covering in this book.

To digress for a moment, suppose our program looked like this.

```
10 LET NAME$ = "Macbeth"
20 PRINT "NAME$"
```

When this program is **RUN**, the computer would do what it always does when asked to **PRINT** something in quotation marks. It would echo the string of characters inside the quotes, and the following would be printed neatly on the screen:

```
RUN

NAME$
```

In the case of our original program (not the digression), that is definitely *not* what we want. We want the computer to **PRINT** the *contents* of the variable called **NAMES**, and that's very different from **PRINT**ing the name of the variable itself.* When a **PRINT** statement is used with a variable, it's as if the contents of the box are shaken out on the screen.

---

*For those of you who tried (in the last chapter) to use **PRINT** statements without beginning quotes, the results you got may now make sense. Although we didn't mention it at the time, the computer may have thought the words following the **PRINT** command were numeric variables. When it tried to **PRINT** the contents of these "variables," zeros appeared on the screen since a value had never been assigned to them in the beginning.

Here's a rule, carved in stone, that is fitting for this occasion: *Never surround variable names with quotation marks when PRINTing them.* Or: "Think before you quote."

Now that we've alerted you to all the potential pitfalls, let's **LIST** our original program.

```
LIST

10 LET NAME$ = "Macbeth"
20 PRINT NAME$
```

Notice that Line 20 has *no* quotes. And now let's **RUN** it.

```
RUN

Macbeth
```

That's it. Not terrifically scintillating perhaps, but very predictable. And that's a goal a programmer should always strive to reach. If the computer can only take orders from you (no variations will ever originate spontaneously from those circuits), then you, of all people, should *never* be surprised by anything that you see on the screen. After all, what you see on the screen could only have come from the instructions *you* programmed. Right?

When you are surprised by something that comes out of a program, then it seems as if the computer knows what you're doing, but you don't! So, if you closely examine the program you are writing, the results will always be predictable. And that way you always know what you're getting and, hopefully, can always get what you want.

Suppose we wanted a little more than just Macbeth's illustrious name printed all alone on the screen. Let's rewrite Line 20 so that the screen displays

```
20 PRINT "My name is ";NAME$;"."
```

If you're having a little trouble figuring out what's going on here, we'll wait while you go back and take a peek at that **PRINT** statement in Chapter 3 about the 90 pencils and 18 pens. The two statements are really very similar. (Notice the space within the quotes after the word *is*.) The only difference in this one is that instead of having a math problem surrounded by semicolons, we have a variable surrounded by semicolons. You see, like straight math problems, a variable in a **PRINT** statement needs semicolon "buffers."

When Line 20 is executed, the word "Macbeth" will be printed out after the word "is" and before the period. In this statement, as in all **PRINT** statements, each string of characters *within* the quotation marks (*My name is _____.*) will be echoed on the screen, and the contents of the variable **NAME$** (Macbeth) will be plugged into the sentence when the program is **RUN**. Watch!

```
RUN

My name is Macbeth.
```

Now, let's **LIST** this program and then see how we can add to it.

```
LIST

10 LET NAME$ = "Macbeth"
20 PRINT "My name is ";NAME$;"."
```

Just for some excitement, let's create a variable called **SPOUSE$**, put it on Line 30, and set it equal to *Lady Macbeth.*

```
30 LET SPOUSE$ = "Lady Macbeth"
```

Don't forget to put the quotes around *Lady Macbeth.* And since there's no sense in creating a variable if you're not going to have the computer display it, we need a **PRINT** statement somewhere for **SPOUSE$**. Let's try

```
40 PRINT "My spouse is ";SPOUSE$;"."
```

That looks very much like the format in Line 20. Now let's add the following line:

```
50 PRINT SPOUSE$;" likes to plot and scheme."
```

Notice that Line 50 does *not* have any quotation marks right after **PRINT** because the first thing to be **PRINT**ed is a variable, not a string of characters (that is, a sentence part). The semicolon, as usual, is used as a buffer. In this case, however, there is only one semicolon. Since **SPOUSE$** has text adjacent to it only on the right side, that is the only place where the "fence" is needed.

Before we add anything else let's **LIST** our program.

```
LIST

10 LET NAME$ = "Macbeth"
20 PRINT "My name is ";NAME$;"."
30 LET SPOUSE$ = "Lady Macbeth"
40 PRINT "My spouse is ";SPOUSE$;"."
50 PRINT SPOUSE$;" likes to plot and scheme."
```

And now let's **RUN** it.

```
RUN

My name is Macbeth.
My spouse is Lady Macbeth.
Lady Macbeth likes to plot and scheme.
```

Although it reads like a Shakespearean primer, our program *is* working and that's the most important part.

Now let's create a somewhat different program. We'll reuse **NAME$**, this time assigning it the string *Count Dracula*. Since the Count never took a wife, let's give him an animal companion instead by creating a variable called **ANIMAL$**. Let's also create a variable that will store the animal's name, and call it **PETNAME$**.* Finally, we'll describe the preferred activities of the animal with a variable called **VERB$**.

This is what we have in mind.

```
NEW

10 LET NAME$ = "Count Dracula"
20 PRINT "My name is ";NAME$;"."
30 LET ANIMAL$ = "tarantula"
40 LET PETNAME$ = "Brunhilda"
50 PRINT "My ";ANIMAL$;" is ";PETNAME$;"."
60 LET VERB$ = "spin"
70 PRINT PETNAME$;" likes to ";VERB$;"."
```

Let's **RUN** it now.

```
RUN

My name is Count Dracula.
My tarantula is Brunhilda.
Brunhilda likes to spin.
```

By rewriting the **LET** statements on lines 10, 30, 40, and 60, we can create a program that looks like this

```
10 LET NAME$ = "Gandalf"
20 PRINT "My name is ";NAME$;"."
30 LET ANIMAL$ = "horse"
```

---

*We purposely did not use **NAME$** again because a variable can only hold one "value" at a time. A new value assigned to an old variable replaces the old value. For example, if you **RUN**

```
10 LET FOOD$ = "spaghetti"
20 LET FOOD$ = "ravioli"
30 PRINT FOOD$
```

the word *ravioli* will be printed on the screen because Line 20 replaces the old value in **FOOD$**.

```
40 LET PETNAME$ = "Shadowfax"
50 PRINT "My ";ANIMAL$;" is ";PETNAME$;"."
60 LET VERB$ = "gallop at light speed"
70 PRINT PETNAME$;" likes to ";VERB$;"."
```

and **RUN**s like this.

```
RUN

My name is Gandalf.
My horse is Shadowfax.
Shadowfax likes to gallop at light speed.
```

There is no limit to the way your imagination can use variables in a program. As you can see, the hardest thing about programming string variables is remembering the dollar sign (**$**), the quotation marks, and the semicolons. But just like learning to drive a car with a standard transmission, it all becomes second nature to you with practice.

Before we move on to the section covering numeric variables, we are going to give you a little mid-term quiz to check your understanding of what we've covered so far. Some questions have multiple answers.

1. When naming a string variable, make sure the last character in the name is a:
   a. period
   b. letter S
   c. dollar sign

2. Which of the following are acceptable names for string variables?
   a. **ADDRESS$**
   b. **HEIGHT**
   c. **RACE$**
   d. **AGE**

3. Which line correctly assigns a value to a string variable?
   ```
   10 LET NAME = "Portia"
   20 LET NAME$ = Ophelia
   30 LET NAME$ = "Gertrude"
   ```

4. When text and a variable are both included in a **PRINT** statement, they must be separated by a:

    a. semicolon
    b. hyphen
    c. dollar sign
    d. double yellow line

TRYING IT WITH NUMBERS

Once you know how to use string variables, using numeric variables is a breeze. We've got a program here that we're going to unveil to you step-by-step. Hopefully, when we get to the last step, you will know everything there is to know about numeric variables as well.

A string variable, as we said at the beginning of this chapter, is used to store *anything* (letters, punctuation marks, special symbols, or numbers). Now, if we can put numbers in a string variable, why do we need numeric variables at all? Simply because string variables *cannot be used for calculations.*

Just as the distinction between a number and a letter is erased when either is put inside the quotation marks of a **PRINT** statement, the distinction between them is also erased when either is put in a string variable. In other words, a number in a numeric variable can be mathematically contorted in any possible way, but a number in a string variable has the same non-mathematical status as a "q," "," or "&."

Most people find computing an unproductive experience if they are not working at something practical (for shame, using a computer to play Space Invaders). We thought it would be appropriate to demonstrate the concept of variables in a very down-to-earth way.

Since many computer programs are somewhat math-oriented, we have put together a little program that uses numeric variables and that will extol the virtues of "growing your own." We call it "The Chicken and The Egg Program."

As with string variables, whenever you wish to put some data into a numeric variable, you use the **LET** command. Let's start with the following:

```
NEW

10 LET EGGS = 36
```

Unlike string variables, however, the contents of a numeric variable are *never* enclosed in quotes. If we were to **RUN** this program right now, what do you think we'd see on the screen? **SYNTAX ERROR**, or the number 36 perhaps? Let's try it and see.

```
RUN
```

As we said during our discussion of string variables, the **LET** command only allows us to put something in a variable; it won't display anything on the screen. If we want the computer to display the *contents* of **EGGS** on the screen (and this is no yolk), we need to tell it to **PRINT EGGS**. Let's go ahead and add that command to the program on Line 20.

```
20 PRINT EGGS
```

Remember, don't put any quotation marks around **EGGS**. It's a variable, not a string of characters to be **PRINT**ed.

Now we're ready to **LIST** and **RUN** the program.

```
LIST

10 LET EGGS = 36
20 PRINT EGGS

RUN

36
```

Now that we understand how this works, we can expand the program and really jazz it up. The nicest thing about a variable is that you can play around with it. Suppose, for example, we change the variable **EGGS** to represent the number of eggs three chickens can lay in a week. If we want the output portion of our program to be more informative, we could rewrite Line 20 so it looks like this.

```
20 PRINT "Our chickens lay ";EGGS;" eggs each week."
```

Line 20 is really not that difficult to interpret when you look at each part separately. The first element "Our chickens lay" is, of course, a string with its own private opening and closing quotes. The second element is the variable **EGGS**, which is offset on each side by semicolons. Then all that's left of this **PRINT** statement is the string "eggs each week." You've got it. That's the whole thing.

When we **LIST** this program, the new Line 20 will, of course, take the place of the old Line 20. Look!

```
LIST

10 LET EGGS = 36
20 PRINT "Our chickens lay ";EGGS;" eggs each week."
```

Now let's **RUN** it.

```
RUN

Our chickens lay 36 eggs each week.
```

Very good. That wasn't so hard, was it? Now suppose over a period of four or five weeks the chickens slack off and the average number of eggs laid by the three of them drops to 27. How could we get our program to reflect the change? It's really rather simple because we only have to rewrite the **LET** statement on Line 10.

Here's the new Line 10 to enter into the program.

```
10 LET EGGS = 27
```

By re**RUN**ning the program now you will see

```
RUN

Our chickens lay 27 eggs each week.
```

Let's suppose we wanted to make this program even *more* flexible. How would we do it? Right now in this program three pieces of data have the potential of being varied. They are: the number of eggs, the number of chickens, and the number of weeks. We've already created a variable that is handling the first one; so now let's take care of the second, the number of chickens. With an unprecedented spark of originality, we will call this variable **CHICKENS**.

Since the computer has to know what **CHICKENS** is equal to *before* it can **PRINT** it, we have to set the value of **CHICKENS** somewhere *before* Line 20. Let's do it on Line 15. When you've typed in the new line, the program listing should look like this.

 Our lay OOOOOOOO each week.
OOOOOOOOO
OOOOOOOOO

```
LIST

10 LET EGGS = 27
15 LET CHICKENS = 3
20 PRINT "Our ";CHICKENS;" chickens lay ";EGGS;
   " eggs each week."
```

If you thought the old Line 20 was a bit complicated, you're going to think this new one is a doozy. To understand it, all you need to do is examine it element by element, noting where the quotation marks open and close, and remembering that variables never have quotation marks around them. If that doesn't help, then it's back to the pencils and pens in Chapter 3 for you.

Another thing about Line 20 that's new is the fact that it takes up more than one line on the screen. Even though the variable EGGS may appear at the right edge of our screen, it is *not* the end of the information that we want to put on Line 20. When you're typing any line into the computer, you *never* hit **RETURN** until you're completely finished with the line. Therefore, keep typing.

The computer will take care of everything by automatically going to the beginning of the next line. On Line 20, *don't hit RETURN until the closing quotes after the word "week."*

When this program is **RUN**, the following will be **PRINT**ed on the screen:

```
RUN

Our 3 chickens lay 27 eggs each week.
```

If we get a couple more chickens, we'll have to change Line 15. Let's do that now.

```
15 LET CHICKENS = 5
```

And if we've got more chickens, we'll probably get more eggs. Let's change Line 10 to reflect the increase in egg production.

```
10 LET EGGS = 45
```

We can **LIST** the program now.

```
LIST

10 LET EGGS = 45
15 LET CHICKENS = 5
20 PRINT "Our ";CHICKENS;" chickens lay "; EGGS;
   "eggs each week."
```

Since we're changing the values in **CHICKENS** and in **EGGS**, let's imagine that we are now being kept so busy collecting eggs we don't have time to calculate egg totals on a weekly basis. We'd better do it just once a month. Therefore, let's create a new variable called **WEEKS**. We'll put it on Line 25 and use it to store the number of weeks in the egg-laying period.

```
25 LET WEEKS = 4
```

If we're going to go to the trouble of creating the variable **WEEKS**, we'd better create a new **PRINT** statement. Line 30 will calculate the number of eggs laid during that period (by multiplying the eggs laid in one week by the number of weeks in the period, or **EGGS∗WEEKS**) and display the answer on the screen.

```
30 PRINT "In ";WEEKS;" weeks they can lay ";
   EGGS ∗ WEEKS;" eggs."
```

When we **LIST** the whole program now, it will look like this.

```
LIST

10 LET EGGS = 45
15 LET CHICKENS = 5
20 PRINT "Our ";CHICKENS;" chickens lay ";EGGS;
   " eggs each week."
25 LET WEEKS = 4
30 PRINT "In ";WEEKS;" weeks they can lay ";EGGS*
   WEEKS;" eggs."
```

And when we **RUN** it, this is what you'll get (and we hope you're fond of eggs).

```
RUN

Our 5 chickens lay 45 eggs each week.
In 4 weeks they can lay 180 eggs.
```

That's great. Now, there's one last step to this process. Suppose, instead of just leaving **EGGS*WEEKS** as it is, we take the result and store it in a variable called **AMOUNT**. (By the way, if you have better names for any of these variables, feel free to use them; even [choke] X,Y, or Z would work as well.) If we put **AMOUNT** on Line 27, it would look like this.

```
27 LET AMOUNT = EGGS*WEEKS
```

Now we can rewrite Line 30 so it looks like this.

```
30 PRINT "In ";WEEKS;" weeks they can lay ";AMOUNT;
   " eggs."
```

When we **LIST** the program at this point, we get

```
LIST

10 LET EGGS = 45
15 LET CHICKENS = 5
20 PRINT "Our ";CHICKENS;" chickens lay ";EGGS;
   " eggs each week."
25 LET WEEKS = 4
27 LET AMOUNT = EGGS*WEEKS
30 PRINT "In ";WEEKS;" weeks they can lay ";AMOUNT;
   " eggs."
```

The new Line 30 does not really represent a significant change in the program; it just makes the line more compact. In fact, when we **RUN** it, the screen output is exactly the same as it was before.

```
RUN

Our 5 chickens lay 45 eggs each week.
In 4 weeks they can lay 180 eggs.
```

Cheaper by the Dozen

The reason we created the variable called **AMOUNT** is so that we would be able to do a little more math just a little more easily. If, for example, we wanted to figure out how many dozens of eggs were being produced every four weeks in that hen house of ours (hold on to your math phobias), we'd need to multiply the number of eggs times the number of weeks and divide them by 12; or, **EGGS*WEEKS/12**.

But wait! Didn't we just say on Line 27 that **AMOUNT = EGGS*WEEKS**? Sure we did. So you would have to be a real sadist to make the poor

computer go ahead and figure out **EGGS∗WEEKS** again. Now let's be practical. Which of the following lines makes more sense? Which is the better Line 40 for our program?

```
40 LET DOZENS = EGGS*WEEKS/12
```

or

```
40 LET DOZENS = AMOUNT/12
```

The first one you say? Oh. Well, this is *not* a quiz so you will be given two guesses. The second one you say? That's absolutely correct! The second one is better because you not only succeeded in getting the computer to do the job in the least possible number of steps, you also made the program more readable for us humans.

The more steps the computer has to take, the more time it needs to take them—that is, the longer the program will take to execute. In a program like ours, we might be talking about 0.023448 second versus 0.023447 second, but in very long and involved programs the time difference could be considerable.

So remember folks, although the computer certainly wouldn't mind multiplying **EGGS∗WEEKS** for you on Line 27 and then again on Line 40, why would anyone want it to?

Now that you understand the rules of the game, there's one other line we're going to add here before we **LIST** and **RUN** the whole program. It is a final **PRINT** statement on Line 50.

```
50 PRINT "And that makes ";DOZENS;" dozen eggs!"
```

We need Line 50 in the program because, without the **PRINT** command, results (calculations and so forth) are never displayed on screen.

Now, let's **LIST** this monstrosity before it gets any longer.

```
LIST

10 LET EGGS = 45
15 LET CHICKENS = 5
20 PRINT "Our ";CHICKENS;" chickens lay ";EGGS;
   " eggs each week."
25 LET WEEKS = 4
27 LET AMOUNT = EGGS*WEEKS
30 PRINT "In ";WEEKS;" weeks they can lay ";AMOUNT;
   " eggs."
40 LET DOZENS = AMOUNT/12
50 PRINT "And that makes ";DOZENS;" dozen eggs!"
```

Let's **RUN** it.

```
RUN

Our 5 chickens lay 45 eggs each week.
In 4 weeks they can lay 180 eggs.
And that makes 15 dozen eggs!
```

We'll stop here with this program, but we want you to know that there is literally no end to what can be done with variables.

JUNK MAIL EXPOSED

Finally, we want to talk about what may be the ultimate computer abuse, one that affects each of us every day. We are, of course, referring to junk mail. Every time you open your mail these days, you see computer-printed letters that make use of variables. We've certainly all had the experience of receiving a "personally" addressed letter we knew had been sent to millions of other people.

These little letter-writing programs are getting more and more sophisticated all the time. By this, we mean that they have more and more "personalized" variables in them (and we can only guess where the people who send them are getting all this information about us). Here's an example of what one of these programs might look like.

```
 10 LET NAME$ = "Miranda Veranda"
 20 LET ADDRESS$ = "123 Willowood Road"
 30 LET PET$ = "canary"
 40 LET PRIZE = 350
 50 LET PETAGE = 2
100 PRINT "Dear ";NAME$;","
110 PRINT
120 PRINT "    Congratulations, ";NAME$;","
130 PRINT "we are delighted to tell you about a"
140 PRINT "special prize which is coming to you"
150 PRINT "at your home on ";ADDRESS$;"."
160 PRINT "Yes, you and your ";PET$;", who will"
170 PRINT "soon celebrate his number ";PETAGE;
    " year on"
180 PRINT "this planet, will be receiving a ";PRIZE
190 PRINT "pound bag of Wonderpet ";PET$;" food."
200 PRINT
210 PRINT "    Again, our heartfelt congratula-"
220 PRINT "tions to you, ";NAME$;", and"
230 PRINT "may you and your ";PET$;" enjoy"
240 PRINT "another ";PETAGE*50;" happy years together."
250 PRINT
260 PRINT "Sincerely,"
270 PRINT "Wonderpet Food Company"
```

We've decided that since this is the last program in this chapter, we're not going to RUN it for you. At this stage of the game you *should* be able to look at a program and *know* what the output would look like. (You will be able to see the RUN of this program if you look in the Quiz Answers at the end of the book. Try to visualize it before you look back there.)

See what tomorrow's mail brings (pick out all the variables in any computerized letters you receive) and have fun with what you've learned. This is just the beginning of our study of variables; there's more to come.

SUMMARY

Variables are memory boxes that can be created with the BASIC command LET. Numeric variables are set up to store *only* numbers, and string variables can store *any* characters. As we have seen, variables really are variable, and that's what makes them so useful in programs. For storing pieces of information and for creating, examining, and manipulating relationships between pieces of information, variables come in very handy.

4 QUIZ

Good luck! Quiz questions 1-4 are on pages 81 and 82. Again, some of the questions have *multiple* answers.

5. When creating a numeric variable, make sure that the last character of the name you choose is *not* a:

    a. letter
    b. dollar sign
    c. number

6. Which of the following could *not* be put in a numeric variable?

    a. 14.562
    b. $1,500
    c. Emily Dickinson
    d. 555-1212
    e. -15

7. Which line of the following program has a syntax error?

```
10 LET AGE = 30
20 PRINT AGE;"! You don't look a day over ";AGE-1;"."
30 LET COMMENT$ = Pshaw!
40 PRINT COMMENT$
```

8. Computerized mass mailings obviously make use of:

    a. computers
    b. variables
    c. sticky gummed labels
    d. all of the above

9. Which of the following are acceptable names for numeric variables?

    a. **JAKE**
    b. **PLANT$**
    c. **LETTER**
    d. **WIDTH**
    e. **FOOD$**

10. To change the contents of any variable:

    a. use the **PRESTO CHANGEO** command
    b. reenter the line with the **LET** statement and give the variable a different value
    c. type **NEW**

11. Which statement is correct?

    a. `10 LET NUMBER =` `six little numbers`
    b. `10 LET NUMBER =` `"6"`
    c. `10 LET NUMBER =` `6`

12. String variables and numeric variables *can* be used in the same program: True or False?

13. A program that has the statement **LET FOOD$ = "escargot"** but is missing the statement **PRINT FOOD$** is probably the result of a careless oversight, because the contents of **FOOD$** will never get:

    a. **LIST**ed
    b. **RUN**
    c. changed
    d. displayed

5 INPUT

Teaching the computer how to ask questions

Computer: Welcome to Thorall Gardens. What is your name, please?

Human: Leslie Palmtree.

Computer: I am most delighted to make your acquaintance. Is it Ms. or Mr. Palmtree?

Human: Ms.

Computer: Very good, Ms. Palmtree. May I call you Leslie?

Human: I'm not really sure.

Computer: Yes or no, please, Ms. Palmtree. May I call you Leslie?

Human: Yes.

Computer: Thank you, Leslie! I'm sure this will be the beginning of a wonderful relationship.

What's this, a computer starring in a British-style drawing room comedy? Somewhere after the chickens and the mass mailings, our computer seems to have become a true conversationalist complete with a set of very nice manners! The thing that makes the above dialogue so appealing is that it *is*, in fact, a dialogue—it's *interactive*. Programs that are interactive allow *anyone* (even those with no knowledge of programming) to contribute information necessary to making a program work.

So far, we know how to tell the computer to **PRINT** numbers, letters, and even blank lines on the screen. We have also managed to store specified pieces of information in distinctly labeled boxes called variables, and use them in several different ways.

Everything we've learned has enabled us to put information into the computer and display it on the screen. The only drawback to what we've been programming is that *none of it is interactive.* And because of that fact, the only way we've been able to change data is by rewriting program lines, which can be extremely tedious.

We are about to remedy that situation by learning a BASIC statement that will bring the computer to a new level of "intelligence." With a command called **INPUT**, we'll be teaching the computer to ask questions, accept answers, and respond "intelligently."

ASK ME ANYTHING

The computer really can be programmed to ask a question, and all you have to do is dream one up. By this, we mean that the question itself is the programmer's creation and can be literally anything. For example, "How's your Aunt Margaret?", "Where did you put my tennis racquet?", and "Why weren't you at work yesterday?" are all perfectly legitimate questions to expect from a computer.

If you want to program—that is, teach the computer how to ask—these questions, the first thing you have to do is enclose each one within quotation marks in a **PRINT** statement. Big deal. We learned that in Chapter 2.

True, but there is a vast difference between getting the computer to display a question and getting it to *ask* a question and *wait* for and accept an answer. Take the following program, for example:

```
NEW

10 PRINT "What is your name?"
20 PRINT "What is your favorite color?"
30 PRINT "What size T-shirt do you wear?"
```

If we **RUN** this one, we will get

```
RUN

What is your name?
What is your favorite color?
What size T-shirt do you wear?
```

Are these questions? Sure they are. But there is something missing here. If these questions are going to be displayed on the computer's screen, when will anyone get a chance to answer them? In other words, when a question is asked, we expect an answer to follow.

When a program consisting of a series of **PRINT** statements is **RUN**, the computer zips through every one of them without pausing for anyone or anything (except syntax errors, which always stop a computer dead in its tracks). So just programming questions in the form of **PRINT** statements is not going to do it. The only way to give a human the opportunity to respond to a question on a computer is to program the computer to wait and "listen." That is done with the **INPUT** command.

The Computer, the Programmer, and
The Rest of the World

In the last chapter we had a program that began with

```
10 LET NAME$ = "Count Dracula"
20 PRINT "My name is ";NAME$;"."
```

And when we ran it, we got

```
My name is Count Dracula.
```

Forever more, whenever this program is **RUN**, the name will *always* be Count Dracula. (Getting rid of him will be only slightly easier than plunging a stake in his heart.) We could change the name in **NAMES** by rewriting Line 10. Yes, we could do that. But suppose we had the computer do it for us. Sound intriguing?

Let's create a new program that is a slight modification of the old program. What we have in mind will hardly be earth shattering in appearance; but, in capability, it will be far more sophisticated than the elegant Count Dracula.

We will, as usual, begin with Line 10.

```
NEW

10 PRINT "Hello, what is your name";
```

Line 10 should hardly look unique at this point in the game (after all, this is Chapter 5). It is an ordinary **PRINT** statement and will, when **RUN**, dutifully display its string of characters on the screen. After the close of the quotation marks there is a lone semicolon and that is a bit unusual. If you remember from Chapters 3 and 4, the semicolon always tells the computer that there's more to come. The semicolon *connects* the **PRINT** statement on Line 10 with the **INPUT** statement on Line 20. The **INPUT** statement looks like this.

```
20 INPUT NAME$
```

Line 20 may not look like much, but it sets up an *answer box* for the question, "What is your name?" It is an **INPUT** statement and consists of the **INPUT** command and the string variable **NAME$**.

Remember the following: *A **PRINT** statement that asks a question is always followed by an **INPUT** statement with a variable.*

If the answer to the question is going to be a number, use a numeric variable. If the answer is going to be anything else, you have to use a string variable.

The program ends with Line 30.

```
30 PRINT "Nice to meet you, ";NAME$;"."
```

Line 30 is a **PRINT** statement that will display a polite salutation to the user, addressing him or her by name.

Let's **LIST** this program so we can see what all the parts look like.*

```
LIST

10 PRINT "Hello, what is your name";
20 INPUT NAME$
30 PRINT "Nice to meet you, ";NAME$;"."
```

When we **RUN** this program something very interesting occurs. We get

```
RUN

Hello, what is your name? ■
```

The computer displays the question (this shouldn't come as any surprise since we asked the computer to **PRINT** it), a space, and our omnipresent friend the cursor. The little white box on the screen (see Chapter 3) is poised

---

*Remember, if you are using a BASIC that requires your string variables to be DIMensioned (like Atari BASIC), do so at the beginning of the program.

expectantly at the end of the line. (We have purposely inserted this space to the left of the cursor for clarity. Most computers will not automatically display this space.)

Notice that a question mark has mysteriously appeared after the word "name." You might wonder where it came from, since it was not included on Line 10. The answer is simply this: *In most BASICs, whenever the* **INPUT** *command is used, a question mark will be displayed on the screen when the program is* **RUN**.

Since this free question mark will always accompany **INPUT**, you don't need to put a question mark at the end of the question on a **PRINT** line. If you forget and put it in anyway, the computer will display two question marks following your question when the program is **RUN**.

Is Anybody There

So here's the question on the screen.

```
Hello, what is your name? ∎
```

And now you may be wondering why the computer seems to be in a state of suspended animation. Why doesn't it move on to the **PRINT** statement on Line 30, like it always does? Because it's waiting for some *human interaction*. You see, when you use **INPUT** in a program, nothing will follow the asking of a question until an answer (any answer) is typed in and the **RETURN** key is pressed.

Now that we know the computer is waiting for us to answer the question, let's not keep it waiting any longer. (**NOTE**: The computer's part in all of our interactive programs is printed in black type. Your answers, which will always be arbitrary, are printed in color).

```
Hello, what is your name? Scarlett O'Hara
Nice to meet you, Scarlett O'Hara.
```

Very interesting. Something is definitely different here. Let's try it again and see if we can figure it out.

```
RUN

Hello, what is your name? Winston Churchill
Nice to meet you, Winston Churchill.
```

Every time we **RUN** this program, the only things that remain the same are the opening question, and the phrase "Nice to meet you". The **INPUT** command automatically takes what you type as the answer and places it in its variable (**NAMES**, in this case). In other words, whatever we type in as our "name" is what the computer will use to address us. Very clever.

But what would happen if we typed in something that could not, by any stretch of the imagination, be construed as a name? Will the computer be smart enough to catch us?

```
RUN

Hello, what is your name? a4%Tn
Nice to meet you, a4%Tn.
```

Hmmm. Just as we suspected. Garbage in and garbage out. The computer asks a question and echoes the response. The program is interactive, but the computer, unfortunately (or fortunately, depending on your point of view), is still not any smarter than it has ever been. It just appears more intelligent because it seems to be "talking" to us. Now that we've seen the results and have an understanding of how that new **INPUT** command actually works, let's **LIST** the program once again.

```
LIST

10 PRINT "Hello, what is your name";
20 INPUT NAME$
30 PRINT "Nice to meet you, ";NAME$;"."
```

Lines 10 and 20, with the semicolon between them, are working together. They tell the computer, "Ask the question 'What is your name?' and, when you receive an answer from the human at the keyboard, store it in variable **NAMES**." And that is exactly what happens every time the program is **RUN**.

Some people get confused when they are creating the **PRINT**ed text for **INPUT** statements. They often feel compelled to immediately type in an answer to the question they've just finished writing. There are *no answers* in this program. There are only *questions* and *answer boxes*. This is an essential distinction.

To fully understand how the **INPUT** statement works you must take the point of view of the playwright who is producing a script for the computer. The only time that you, or anyone else, will have the opportunity to answer the questions is when the program is **RUN**. Rushing the curtain time will only result in syntax errors (and bad reviews).

Now back to our program. After the question is asked and answered, what happens to the answer? That's where Line 30 comes in. It is simply a **PRINT** statement containing a string of characters and a variable. It is responsible for **PRINT**ing out the phrase "Nice to meet you," and plugging the previously given answer into that phrase. There you have the trick behind the "magic." The computer appears to have listened very attentively and responded appropriately.

Adding More Questions

Now that we know how it works, let's program some more questions.

```
40 PRINT "Where do you live";
50 INPUT PLACE$
60 PRINT "What do you do for a living";
70 INPUT JOB$
```

These lines will ask the user where the person lives and what he or she does for a living. Please remember that neither **PLACE$** nor **JOB$** is an *answer* to anything. They are answer boxes and nothing more. They will remain empty until the user fills them. So far, with these additional four lines, all we have created is two more questions as well as two more answer boxes.

To create a simulation of a dialogue, a **PRINT** statement is needed to display the user's answer in an appropriate response. We already have a **PRINT** statement for our **NAME$** variable (Line 30), so let's create a **PRINT** statement for **PLACE$** and **JOB$** and put it on Line 80.

```
80 PRINT "What a coincidence, ";NAME$;", my uncle also
   works at ";JOB$;" in ";PLACE$;"."
```

This line will plug all three variables (**NAME$**, **PLACE$**, and **JOB$**) into a sentence.

Let's **LIST** this now and put all the pieces together.

```
LIST

10 PRINT "Hello, what is your name";
20 INPUT NAME$
30 PRINT "Nice to meet you, ";NAME$;"."
40 PRINT "Where do you live";
50 INPUT PLACE$
60 PRINT "What do you do for a living";
70 INPUT JOB$
80 PRINT "What a coincidence, ";NAME$;", my uncle also
   works at ";JOB$;" in ";PLACE$;"."
```

And now for a **RUN**.

```
RUN

Hello, what is your name? Nero
Nice to meet you, Nero.
Where do you live? Rome
What do you do for a living? music
What a coincidence, Nero. My uncle also works at music
in Rome.
```

Our program is looking very professional. Under our guidance, the computer can ask intelligent questions and respond to the user with the attentiveness of a good friend.

GOTO—Directing the Computer from Within the Program

We'd like, at this point, to introduce a simple new command that will make your life as a programmer much easier. Surely you've noticed that whenever we want to try the program *one more time,* we use **RUN**. The time has come to let you know that there's another way to do it.

Let's say, for example, you want to use **INPUT** to create a program with a series of questions to be answered by several different users. When each person has finished, how would you start the next person on Question Number 1?

You could stand by the computer and type **RUN** after each user has answered the final question, or you could tell each user to type **RUN** when he or she first sits down at the computer. Better still, with a command called **GOTO**, you could instruct the computer to return to the first line of the program and ask each question again.

Let's take our last program, the one with the variables **NAME$**, **PLACE$**, and **JOB$**, and do two things: Add a Line 90 to **PRINT** a blank line that separates the end of one series of questions from the beginning of another; and add a Line 100 with a **GOTO** command.

```
90 PRINT
100 GOTO 10
```

The **GOTO** command is always followed by a line number so the computer

---

The Expanded INPUT Command

In most versions of Microsoft BASIC, the computer can be programmed to ask questions without using the **PRINT** command at all. In these cases, the text of the question can be placed within quotes in an **INPUT** command, like this.

```
10 INPUT "Hello, what is your name";NAME$
```

This capability allows the programmer to use fewer steps in the program, and that means less typing. There is a drawback, though. If, for example, the computer asks, "What is your name?" and the user answers, "Wendell," you would have difficulty getting the computer to then say, "How old are you, Wendell?" You couldn't do it by entering

```
10 INPUT "Hello, what is your name";NAME$
20 INPUT "How old are you, ";NAME$;AGE
```

because "Wendell" would be stored in one variable (**NAME$**) and Wendell's age would need to be stored in a second variable (**AGE**). This is not going to work for the following reason: *An **INPUT** statement cannot be used to **PRINT** the contents of one variable while it requests information to fill another variable.*

If you do want to use an earlier variable in a later question, you would have to change the program so that you get

```
10 INPUT "Hello, what is your name";NAME$
20 PRINT "How old are you, ";NAME$;
30 INPUT AGE
```

Granted, it looks awkward, but if you want to personalize your questions, that's the way you would have to do it.

knows exactly *where* you want it to go. Line 100 says, "Go to Line 10 and, when you get there, execute the command." The computer will return to Line 10, execute the command, and from there go to Line 20 and do what needs to be done there. From Line 20, the computer will proceed to Line 30, then to Line 40, and so forth, until it gets to Line 100. Of course, Line 100 says "Go to 10..." and so the computer will, again and again and again, in an endless *loop.* *

Let's **LIST** the program and see what it looks like with the addition of these two lines.

```
LIST

 10 PRINT "Hello, what is your name";
 20 INPUT NAME$
 30 PRINT "Nice to meet you, ";NAME$;"."
 40 PRINT "Where do you live";
 50 INPUT PLACE$
 60 PRINT "What do you do for a living";
 70 INPUT JOB$
 80 PRINT "What a coincidence, ";NAME$;", my uncle also
    works at ";JOB$;" in ";PLACE$;"."
 90 PRINT
100 GOTO 10
```

---

*The only way out of a loop is with the interrupt key on the computer's keyboard. Common interrupt keys are **BREAK**, control **c** (press "**c**" while holding down the key labeled **CTRL**), and **RESET**. To find out which key has that function on your computer, check the user's manual.

When we **RUN** the program now, we get

```
RUN

Hello, what is your name? Davey Jones
Nice to meet you, Davey Jones.
Where do you live? South Pacific
What do you do for a living? deep sea exploration
What a coincidence, Davey Jones. My uncle also works
at deep sea exploration in South Pacific.

Hello, what is your name? Lady Godiva
Nice to meet you, Lady Godiva.
Where do you live? Coventry
What do you do for a living? exhibitionism
What a coincidence, Lady Godiva. My uncle also works
at exhibitionism in Coventry.

Hello, what is your name?

BREAK IN LINE 20
```

If the interrupt key is pressed, **BREAK IN LINE 20** (or a similar message) is **PRINT**ed on the screen. It tells us where the computer was (in the program) at the time the ax fell. Unless we hit the interrupt key, our program will continue on and on.

One note about the kinds of questions we've been programming here. If the computer were curious, it might ask Lady Godiva if she had ever been arrested while doing her **JOB$**, but since the answer to that question would be "**YES**" or "**NO**," we have to steer clear for now.

Questions requiring **YES** or **NO** can only be dealt with properly using *conditional* responses. If, for example, the computer were to ask, "Do you enjoy science fiction?", we could program it to respond to three possible answers that the user might supply. One for **YES**, one for **NO**, and one for anything other than **YES** and **NO**. These kinds of conditional statements are one step beyond the **INPUT** command, and we'll be examining them in detail in Chapter 6.

Now that we get the gist of **INPUT** statements with string variables, let's try some with numeric variables.

A DIALOGUE WITH NUMBERS

The **INPUT** command can be used to ask any question at all. If the answer to the question is a number, then the variable at the end of the **INPUT** statement is a numeric variable (you knew that). Let's try one with numbers this time. How about a check balancing program? Too complex, you think? Nonsense. We can write a simple check balancing program with just eight lines.

The first thing you do before you ever put your fingers on a computer keyboard to write a program is think about the task to be done. If we want to write a check balancing program, we first divide the task into small sequential steps (see Eggplant Parmesan in Chapter 3). When we get our monthly statement from our bank, we have been thoughtfully provided with a step-by-step, "how to" section on the reverse side.

To have the computer balance our checkbook, all we have to do is create a program that goes through the same process we follow when (and if) we do it manually. After this program is completed and **RUN**, the computer screen will display the same questions as those written on the bank statement and will store the answers in variables.

On our bank statement, Step Number 1 tells us to enter, on the line provided, the ending balance from the front of the statement. Let's create a question for the computer to ask, using **PRINT**, followed by **INPUT** and the variable **BALANCE** set up to store the answer. How about this?

```
NEW

10 PRINT "What is your ending balance";
20 INPUT BALANCE
```

Not very difficult. And, as you can see, the question we created was a fairly obvious one. Now, Step Number 2 on the bank statement says, "Place the total of unposted deposits on Line 2." For those of you who are not hip to the terminology of high finance, "unposted deposits" simply means "money that you have in your account but that we don't show on your statement."

Since we don't know the total of unposted deposits (and neither does the computer at this point), we only need to formulate a question that will enable us to receive the required data. Once again, we use a **PRINT** statement and an **INPUT** statement with a variable. We'd like to use the variable **DEPOSITS**; but since **POS** is a reserved word in some BASICs, we can't. Instead, we'll call our variable **DEP**.

```
30 PRINT "What is your total of unposted deposits";
40 INPUT DEP
```

Now, Step Number 3 of the bank's handy "Beginner's Guide to Balancing Your Checkbook" requires that you fill in the blank with the amount of outstanding checks (meaning, "How much money have you spent from this account that we haven't found out about yet?"). We could pose our third question that same way, but we wouldn't want anyone to think that this book was too informal. Let's just do it this way, using **CHECKS** as the variable that's going to store the answer.

```
50 INPUT "What is your total of outstanding checks";
60 INPUT CHECKS
```

That's the end of the questions that need to be answered, but let's do one more thing before we have the computer calculate our balance. With all of this text on the screen, things are going to look very crowded when we **RUN** this program. Why not have the computer **PRINT** a blank line (on Line 70)? Here it is.

```
70 PRINT
```

Line 70 will serve as a visual separator between the questions on Lines 10 to 60 and the last line of the program.

Now, as the last step of this monthly drudgery, we need to have one line that will make sense out of all the information our user (that lucky individual who will be answering all these questions) will provide. What we need is a **PRINT** statement that will enable the computer to calculate the account balance (by adding what we started with to the deposits we made and subtracting the outstanding checks from the whole thing) and display it on the screen.

```
80 PRINT "Your account balance is ";BALANCE + DEP -
   CHECKS
```

Now, let's **LIST** it and see how much of this the computer has remembered.

```
LIST

10 PRINT "What is your ending balance";
20 INPUT BALANCE
30 INPUT "What is your total of unposted deposits";
40 INPUT DEP
50 INPUT "What is your total of outstanding checks";
60 INPUT CHECKS
70 PRINT
80 PRINT "Your account balance is ";BALANCE + DEP -
   CHECKS
```

That certainly looks like all of it. Let's **RUN**.

```
RUN

What is your ending balance? 500.50
What is your total of unposted deposits? 100.25
What is your total of outstanding checks? 200.00

Your account balance is 400.75
```

Excellent, now let's try that one more time, just for fun.

```
RUN

What is your ending balance? 73.49
What is your total of unposted deposits? 10.50
What is your total of outstanding checks? 187.62

Your account balance is -103.63
```

Oops. Hope we can make it to the bank before it closes.

Negative balance notwithstanding, we have accomplished something quite useful. We've taught the computer to balance a checkbook. (Now if we could only teach it to do the 1040 Form.) Although this program does work, it is far from perfect.

As you may have noticed, in order to answer the questions for the totals of unposted deposits and outstanding checks you have to do some figuring of your own. What kind of computer program would require you to sit there at the keyboard with a little calculator in your hand?

A bare bones model, that's what kind. We had to write the program this way because at this point you folks haven't been taught enough BASIC to do it any other way. The truth is that this program could be modified and expanded to do *all* of the calculations that this check balancing job requires (that includes having the computer ask for the amounts of each of the individual deposits and checks so it can total them itself).

SUMMARY

In this chapter we've learned that there's more than one way to stuff a variable. The special BASIC command **LET** requires information to be programmed in (by the programmer), while **INPUT** permits the user to enter it from the keyboard. In fact, **INPUT** (which is sometimes mistakenly called **IMPUT**) opens new vistas in programming possibilities.

When you use **INPUT**, you are creating a program with more flexibility than you could ever have by using **LET**. Why? Because with an **INPUT** statement, the only thing that is pre-programmed is the question and the answer box (or the place where the answer will be stored). The answers themselves are *never* programmed.

5 QUIZ

1. The **INPUT** statement commands the computer to:
   - *a.* tell a story
   - *b.* answer the phone
   - *c.* accept an answer
   - *d.* sing a song

2. The **LET** command is to **INPUT** as cement is to:
   - *a.* clay
   - *b.* lobster Cantonese
   - *c.* grass
   - *d.* roller skates

3. Which of the following lines contain an error?

```
10 PRINT "What is your favorite hobby";
20 IMPUT HOBBY$
30 PRINT "I've always found ";HOBBY$;" extremely
   dull."
40 PRINT "Where do you go on vacation";
50 INPUT PLACE
60 PRINT "How very strange that someone who likes
   ";HOBBY$;" would also like ";PLACE
```

4. The **LET** and **INPUT** commands can be used in the same program: True or False?

5. The **GOTO 5** command means:
   - *a.* Take 5
   - *b.* Give me 5
   - *c.* Go back to Line 5

6. To stop any program at any time, hit:
   - *a.* the interrupt key
   - *b.* the **RETURN** key
   - *c.* the brakes
   - *d.* all of the above

7. In most BASICs, when creating questions for **INPUT** statements, you don't need to include:
   - *a.* quotation marks
   - *b.* answers
   - *c.* line numbers
   - *d.* question marks

8. The **INPUT** command will never be confused with **IMPUT** if you remember that **INPUT** means:
   - *a.* put in
   - *b.* put up with
   - *c.* put down
   - *d.* put aside

9. Which of the following questions would require more programming skill than you have at this time in order for the computer to give a logical response to the user's answer?
   - *a.* Where were you last night?
   - *b.* What were you doing?
   - *c.* Who was that person I saw you with?
   - *d.* Are you telling the truth?

10. Which line's variable is mismatched with the question it follows?

```
10 PRINT "What is the length, in inches, of the Eiffel
   Tower";
20 INPUT TWER
```

```
30 PRINT "What is your mother's maiden name";
40 INPUT NAME$
50 INPUT "How many legs does a caterpillar have";
60 INPUT LEGS
70 INPUT "What kind of dressing comes with the salad";
80 INPUT DRESSING
```

6 IF/THEN

Conditional statements

We have now taught our dull-witted sailor how to ask questions that start with who, what, where, and when. To complete his education, we need to find a way to teach him to deal with questions starting with can, are, will, and do. All of these questions will require the user to respond with "yes" or "no."

Consequently, these kinds of questions can't be programmed in the same way as the "regular" questions of Chapter 5. This is because the answers to such questions cannot be used effectively with single pre-programmed computer responses. This same problem will arise with any question that leaves the user open to answer in any way he or she likes. Here's what we mean.

Suppose you programmed a computer to ask the question, "How are you?" and **PRINT** the answer (whatever it is) along with the phrase, "Glad to hear it." The program would look like this.

```
NEW

10 PRINT "How are you";
20 INPUT ANSWER$
30 PRINT ANSWER$;"?  Glad to hear it!"
```

Now, we can **RUN** it and see what happens.

```
RUN

How are you? Great
Great?  Glad to hear it!
```

As you can see, everything would work out splendidly as long as the answers received were along the lines of "good," "fine," and "OK." But if, by some chance, the user happened to be someone who had just gotten his wisdom teeth extracted, "Lousy? Glad to hear it!" is not a very appropriate response.

We're going to have to rewrite the program so it can handle the unexpected if we don't want the unfortunate dental patient to think the computer is an insensitive lout.

THE COMPUTER IS REALLY LISTENING

As we learned in Chapter 5, when you use the **INPUT** command, you need a user to interact with the program. It should be noted that users are free agents and are, by nature, an unpredictable lot. And although one can never program a computer with a comeback for every possible human response, a programmer can provide other script options and direct the computer to use them only under certain conditions.

To create the effect of a computer who is really "listening" to a user's answers, we will, in this chapter, teach you to write an interactive program that takes all possible user input into consideration. To demonstrate how this is done, let's begin with a simple question that could be answered by an even more simple "yes" or "no." For example,

```
NEW

10 PRINT "Do you like ice cream";
20 INPUT ANSWER$
```

If we **RUN** the program at this point we will get

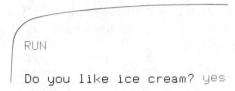

```
RUN

Do you like ice cream? yes
```

That's the end of the program. It doesn't do much, but it did everything we told it to do. It instructs the computer to ask the question and store the answer. Unlike the programs we wrote in Chapter 5, the computer was never told to **PRINT** the variable (**ANSWER$**), and so, after the answer is typed in, the word "yes" is never displayed on the screen again.

Now, suppose we want to have the computer *do* something with the answer that is being stored in **ANSWER$**. Since "Do you like ice cream?" is a question that can be answered with yes or no, it looks like there ought to be two separate responses that the computer can use depending on what **ANSWER$** contains. What we need is a *conditional statement*. This is a line in a program that tells the computer to distinguish between one value and another and then to do something only if a predefined situation occurs.

In our ice cream program, if the user answers the question with "yes," let's tell the computer to **PRINT** the phrase, "So do I." Conversely, if the user says "no," let's instruct the computer to **PRINT** the phrase, "Good. I'll take yours." To put all of that into BASIC, we use what's called an **IF/THEN** statement. Here's what it looks like.

```
30 IF ANSWER$ = "yes" THEN PRINT "So do I."
40 IF ANSWER$ = "no" THEN PRINT "Good.  I'll take
   yours."
```

The construction of Lines 30 and 40 is very specific and should be studied carefully. Each line contains a *conditional statement* and begins with **IF**. (Notice that, other than a line number, *nothing* precedes **IF**. Resist all temptations and similar urges to stick **PRINT**, **INPUT**, or **LET** in front of **IF**.) After **IF** comes the name of the variable whose contents we want the computer to check.

Then comes an equal sign (=) followed by the value with which we want to compare the variable's contents. (In the case of a string variable like **ANSWER$**, the value will *always* be another string. Strings can only be compared with strings and numbers can only be compared with numbers.) The second half of this conditional statement (the word **THEN**) tells the computer what to do **IF** the answer in **ANSWER$** *is* equal to "yes." And **IF** it is, **THEN PRINT** the string, "So do I."

Now, *if* we understand Line 30, *then* Line 40 should be a breeze to interpret. Line 40 tells the computer that **IF** the answer in **ANSWER$** is no, **THEN PRINT**, "Good. I'll take yours." Let's **LIST** our program now and look it over.

```
LIST

10 PRINT "Do you like ice cream";
20 INPUT ANSWER$
30 IF ANSWER$ = "yes" THEN PRINT "So do I."
40 IF ANSWER$ = "no" THEN PRINT "Good.  I'll take
   yours."
```

That looks fine. Line 10 displays the question, Line 20 stores the answer, Line 30 tells the computer what to do if the answer is yes, and Line 40 tells it what to do if the answer is no. Now that we know what's supposed to happen, let's **RUN** it, answer the question, and see if the computer is listening.

```
RUN

Do you like ice cream? yes
So do I.
```

So far so good. Now let's try it with a negative response.

```
RUN

Do you like ice cream? no
Good.  I'll take yours.
```

Nice going. This stuff is easy for a veteran programmer like you. Before we bring on the complications, here's one special note to tuck away in your files for future reference: *Any BASIC command can be used after the THEN in a conditional statement.*

In other words, either of the following is perfectly legal*:

```
10 IF ANSWER$ = "celery" THEN LET AGE = 25
20 IF ANSWER$ = "River City" THEN GOTO 100
```

Which Is Correct—YES, Yes, or yes

Let's try our program again and watch what happens when we are not consistent with the spelling of our answer.

```
RUN

Do you like ice cream? YES
```

---

*A few BASICs will allow only a GOTO command to follow THEN.

What's that? No comment from the computer? What could it mean? What happened to "So do I."? Let's find out.

When a computer is asked to compare two strings (as in Line 30), the two strings must match *character for character.* When *all* the characters match, the condition is said to be TRUE and the computer then has the go-ahead it needs to carry out the command. So, didn't we type in "YES," just as the computer expected? Not exactly. The computer was expecting lower case "yes" and we typed in upper case "YES." This is no small difference to the computer: "Y" is not the same as "y."

As you can see, matching characters is crucial in making conditions true and this means matching upper case with upper case and lower case with lower case. When we answered the question with "YES," the computer had nothing to say. Here's what actually happened while the program was RUNning and the computer was executing it line by line.

After the answer was typed in and stored in ANSWER$, the computer read its instructions on Line 30. The instructions told it, "If ANSWER$ is equal to 'yes,' then..." Uh oh, we have a problem here. The computer checks the contents of ANSWER$ and sees the word "YES."

But "YES" is *not* equal to "yes" (even a computer can see that!). Since it is *not* equal, the computer doesn't even look at the rest of Line 30. Why not? Because the condition that we programmed is *not true.* Okay. Where does the computer go from there? Line 40, of course. Pressing ever onward with the desire to serve.

Line 40 tells the computer "If ANSWER$ is equal to 'no,' then..." Oh no, here we go again. The computer checks the contents of ANSWER$ and sees that "YES" is *not* equal to "no." Since it's *not* equal, the computer calls it quits for Line 40 because the *condition* is not true. (This sounds familiar.) Okay. Where does it go from there? Nowhere. Because there's nowhere to go.

The program ends right there. No more lines to execute, no more worlds to conquer. The computer is speechless because we never programmed it to respond to upper case "YES," and as we mentioned way back in Chapter 2, it has no powers of improvisation.

Although the computer's pathway through this program took two whole paragraphs to explain, it is actually performed in a flash. When the program is RUN and the answer to the question is typed in, it takes fractions of a second for the computer to realize that the conditions on Lines 30 and 40 are not true.

Adding Some Flexibility to the Absolute Perfectionist

It all boils down to this: *Computers are picky.* If we want to create a program that will always perform as expected (even at the sight of an upper case letter), we must program it to accept all likely variations of "yes."

This is not as difficult as it may sound. We can do the job by rewriting Line 30, so that it looks like this.

```
30 IF ANSWER$ = "yes" OR ANSWER$ = "YES" OR ANSWER$ =
   "Yes" THEN PRINT "So do I."
```

Line 30 is using the word **OR** to link together three conditions. (Please note the repetitions of the variable name and the equal sign.) When the computer "reads" this line, it will check the contents of **ANSWER$** against each of the three possibilities until it finds any one of them to be true.

Programming a line this way affords the user more leniency because there is no longer just one true answer. If *any one* of the three conditions is true, then the computer will respond by **PRINT**ing out, "So do I."

While we're at it, let's rewrite Line 40 to make it equally flexible.

```
40 IF ANSWER$ = "no" OR ANSWER$ = "NO" OR ANSWER$ =
   "No" THEN PRINT "Good. I'll take yours."
```

It would be a good idea to **LIST** the program at this point and test out all the changes.

```
LIST

10 PRINT "Do you like ice cream";
20 INPUT ANSWER$
30 IF ANSWER$ = "yes" OR ANSWER$ = "YES" OR ANSWER$ =
   "Yes" THEN PRINT "So do I."
40 IF ANSWER$ = "no" OR ANSWER$ = "NO" OR ANSWER$ =
   "No" THEN PRINT "Good. I'll take yours."
```

Now we can **RUN** it.

```
RUN

Do you like ice cream? YES
So do I.
```

And let us not forget the non-ice cream lovers in the audience.

```
RUN

Do you like ice cream? No
Good. I'll take yours."
```

Great, it works. Now that we have our bases covered with yes and no, what do you think will happen if we answer something completely different? Do you think we'll get a syntax error, both answers, or neither answer?

```
RUN

Do you like ice cream? not really
```

Nothing happened! Were you surprised by that? Were you expecting the computer to **PRINT** out its pre-programmed "Good. I'll take..." response? Sorry, but even though "not really" is a negative answer and the first two characters of the string are the same as one of the conditions on Line 40, it's just not close enough.

There's no getting around this one. The string of characters "not really" is just *not* equal to "no" (nor is it equal to "yes," for that matter). Therefore, no conditions on Line 30 or Line 40 are true. And once again, the computer finds itself on stage without a script.

We could actually get around this one by using the word **OR** and creating the following line:

```
50 IF ANSWER$ = "not really" OR ANSWER$ = "hardly ever"
   OR ANSWER$ = "not on your life" THEN PRINT "Good.
   I'll take yours."
```

Although this line of logic would work (it really would), we think this is getting a bit ridiculous. Come to think of it, the same goes for Lines 30 and 40. (The truth is, someone who wanted to could type in YES or YEs and blow the whole thing anyway.) As a programmer (even a psychic one), you'll *never* be able to predict and program *all* possible answers. So let's not even bother. Besides, we have a much better way.

WHAT TO DO IF, AND WHAT TO DO IF NOT

As we have seen, we encounter some difficulty in our ice cream program when we try to put anything in ANSWER$ other than our pre-programmed values. There must be some way around this, and indeed there is. If you can tell the machine what to do if something is *true,* it is logical to assume that you can also tell it what to do if something is *not* true. This isn't too much to expect because the computer is, if nothing else, a creature of logic.

Since we now know it has the capability, let's write a line for our program that tells the machine what to do if ANSWER$ is *not* equal to "yes" and is also *not* equal to "no." Here it is.

```
50 IF ANSWER$ <> "yes" AND ANSWER$ <> "no" THEN PRINT
   "Next time please answer with yes or no."
```

The unusual symbol (< >) that you see on Line 50 after each occurrence of ANSWER$ is BASIC's "not equal to" symbol. To create it on a computer keyboard, just press the "less than" symbol (<) and put the "greater than" symbol (>) next to it (we'll talk more about these symbols later in this chapter).

Knowing what that symbol means unlocks the mystery of the entire line. Now Line 50 can easily be translated as follows: *If the answer that is being stored in ANSWER$ is not equal to "yes" and the answer that is being stored in ANSWER$ is also not equal to "no," then PRINT the phrase "Next time please answer with yes or no."*

It's certainly a mouthful when you put it that way. But when the computer "reads" the line in BASIC, it will whiz through it faster than an Evelyn Wood honor graduate. Just remember that when you use the word AND, both conditions must be true.

Let's **LIST** the program now and look at it.

```
LIST

10  PRINT "Do you like ice cream";
20  INPUT ANSWER$
30  IF ANSWER$ = "yes" THEN PRINT "So do I."
40  IF ANSWER$ = "no" THEN PRINT "Good. I'll take
    yours."
50  IF ANSWER$ <> "yes" AND ANSWER$ <> "no" THEN PRINT
    "Next time please answer with yes or no."
```

Before we show you what this program does, please notice that we've gone back to our original unadorned versions of Line 30 and Line 40. The reason for this "regression" is that, with the addition of Line 50, the other stuff is not really necessary, although it does make the program more flexible.

Now when we **RUN** the program and answer the question with something other than yes and no, we should get something on the screen besides a blank stare.

```
RUN

Do you like ice cream? sometimes
Next time please answer with yes or no.
```

That's terrific! Now the computer is actually telling us what it needs to go on with the program. (You certainly have to admire a machine that is willing to tell you out front just what it wants.)

How did it happen? It received the answer "sometimes" and first looked at Line 30 to see if the condition was true. It wasn't, so it dropped down to Line 40, where it also met with failure. Now the computer has some place to go after it leaves Line 40.

Line 50 says, "If the answer isn't 'yes' *and* the answer isn't 'no' then..." Well, hurray! shouts the computer. Here's one that fits. "Sometimes" is in

ANSWER$ and it's not the same as "yes" or "no." Both conditions are true and so the computer goes ahead and **PRINT**s

```
Next time please answer with yes or no.
```

A message like that is clear and simple, and one would logically assume that the user would see the error of his ways and respond correctly the second time around. Let's pretend, however, that our user is either the stubborn type with absolutely no intention of complying with the computer's request or the type who never could follow directions.

```
RUN

Do you like ice cream? only on holidays
Next time please answer with yes or no.
```

In a case like this, the computer, unlike its human counterpart, is infinitely patient. It is perfectly willing to ask the question over and over again. It will never raise its voice to the user, and no amount of sarcasm, fury, or exasperation will be in evidence.

Speaking of endless repetitions, this program would be an excellent place to make use of our newly learned **GOTO** command, from Chapter 5. By using **GOTO** at the end of Line 50, we could have the computer automatically loop back to Line 10 and ask the question again without anyone having to type **RUN**.

Here's how we'd add it.

```
50 IF ANSWER$ <> "yes" AND ANSWER$ <> "no" THEN PRINT
   "Next time please answer with yes or no.":GOTO 10
```

That's a colon (:) in front of the **GOTO** command at the end of Line 50. We haven't seen that particular punctuation mark in BASIC before. It translates to "more to come" and allows you to have multiple statements using one line number.

The colon is used whenever you want to add an additional command to a line that already contains a command. As we saw a minute ago, Line 50 was

complete and functional just as it was without the addition of **GOTO**. When we did add **GOTO**, we had to precede it with a colon.*

Another interesting point about adding command statements at the end of conditional (**IF/THEN**) statements is the following: *A command placed at the end of a conditional statement will not (in most BASICs) be executed unless the condition is true.*

In other words, from Line 50, the computer will return to Line 10 if the answer isn't "yes" or "no."

---

*Some BASICs use a backslash (\) instead of a colon to separate multiple statements. Some BASICs don't even allow multiple statements.

Now that we've included Line 50, let's **RUN** the program.

```
RUN

Do you like ice cream? always
Please answer yes or no.
Do you like ice cream? I already said I did!
Please answer yes or no.
Do you like ice cream?
                    ·   (The question will be repeated
                    ·    again and again)
                    ·
Do you like ice cream? yes
So do I.
```

And on and on, until you answer either yes or no to end the program, or stop the **GOTO** loop with the interrupt key (see Chapter 5).

Choosing AND or OR

The difference between the use of **AND** versus **OR** in an **IF/THEN** statement is critical to a program's operation. In case you were wondering if **OR** could be used on Line 50 instead of **AND**, we're going to show you what would happen if the line contained **OR**.

Let's rewrite it now and see what happens.

```
50 IF ANSWER$ <> "yes" OR ANSWER$ <> "no" THEN PRINT
   "Next time please answer with yes or no.":GOTO 10
```

And now let's **LIST** the whole program.

```
LIST

10 PRINT "Do you like ice cream";
20 INPUT ANSWER$
30 IF ANSWER$ = "yes" THEN PRINT "So do I."
40 IF ANSWER$ = "no" THEN PRINT "Good.  I'll take
   yours."
50 IF ANSWER$ <> "yes" OR ANSWER$ <> "no" THEN PRINT
   "Next time please answer with yes or no.":GOTO 10
```

Okay, let's give it a whirl.

```
RUN

Do you like ice cream? yes
So do I.
Next time please answer yes or no.
Do you like ice cream?

BREAK IN LINE 20
```

Wait a minute. Let's interrupt that one and see what happened. We answered "yes" and the computer gave us our predicted yes response, but it didn't stop there as it did before. Instead, we also got the "Next time please..." answer (and the question again) as if we hadn't answered yes at all.

Very interesting. We've got a *bug* here (an undesirable result). We need to take this step by step and see if we can decipher the reason behind the computer's "mistake."

We ran the program, the question was displayed, and the computer waited for our answer. We typed in "yes" and hit **RETURN**. The computer took the "yes" and stored it in **ANSWER$**. It then proceeded to Line 30 and checked to see if the condition was true. It was ("yes" *is* equal to "yes") and so it **PRINT**ed, "So do I."

From there our computer went to Line 40 and checked to see if this condition was true. Sorry, "yes" is not equal to "no" so it cannot **PRINT** "Good. I'll take yours." (and it didn't).

Now this is where the unexpected happened, so pay close attention. Still storing the string "yes" safely in **ANSWERS**, the computer sees Line 50. The key to understanding **OR** is that if *either* condition is true, the statement will execute. The first condition to be checked here says, "If the answer is *not* 'yes.'..." Well, the computer knows that "yes" *is* equal to "yes," and therefore this condition is false.

Next, the computer sees **OR**. The word **OR** means that, even if the first condition is false, the computer still has to check out the second condition to see if it is true. When the computer does this, it sees that the second condition says, "If the answer is not 'no.'...".

Ah ha! The "yes" is *not equal* to "no." So the condition is true! And since it is, the computer **PRINTS** out "Next time..." and loops back to Line 10 where it asks the question again. It isn't what we wanted it to do, but it is, undeniably, what we told it to do.

So there you have it in a coconut shell. *When you use AND, all conditions must be true. When you use OR, only one condition needs to be true.* Now you know why using **AND** makes this program work and using **OR** doesn't.*

IF YOU CAN DO IT WITH WORDS THEN YOU CAN DO IT WITH NUMBERS

The idea behind using numeric variables with conditional statements is the same as using string variables. The only difference is that, in addition to the equal sign (=) and the not equal sign (< >) we used extensively in the string variable section, two other signs are available to us. They are "greater than" (>) and "less than" (<).†

---

*A series of ANDs and ORs can be combined in the same statement to create very complicated conditions. We won't be exploring conditional statements at this level in this book.

† Less than (<) and greater than (>) actually can be used with strings. They will compare the relative position in the alphabet of any letters. For example, "C" is less than "J." This method can be used for alphabetizing.

Here's how they might be used in a program.

```
NEW

10 PRINT "What is the sum of 7 + 6";
20 INPUT ANSWER
30 IF ANSWER > 13 THEN PRINT "Try a smaller number."
   :GOTO 10
40 IF ANSWER < 13 THEN PRINT "Try a larger number."
   :GOTO 10
50 PRINT "That's absolutely correct!"
```

Before we **RUN** this, are there any questions? Yes, you in the green sweater, are you wondering about the **GOTO** that appears on Lines 30 and 40? As we said earlier in this chapter, when you add a **GOTO** command (or any other command, for that matter) at the end of another statement, **GOTO** must be preceded by a colon.

As to the function of the **GOTO**, it is this: When the number stored in **ANSWER** is either less than or greater than 13, the computer will **PRINT** out a hint for the user and return to Line 10 where the question will be asked again and again until the correct answer is given.

Let's try it.

```
RUN

What is the sum of 7 + 6? 14
Try a smaller number.
What is the sum of 7 + 6? 12
Try a larger number.
What is the sum of 7 + 6? 13
That's absolutely correct!
```

As you can see, when the number we entered (14) was larger than 13, the condition on Line 30 was true. What did the computer do then? It **PRINT**ed the feedback phrase "Try a smaller number" and looped back to Line 10 where it asked the question again.

The second time through the program, we entered 12 as our answer. The computer stored it in **ANSWER** and proceeded to Line 30 to check whether the condition was true. It was not, 12 is not greater than 13, so there was no sense hanging around.

In an act of great determination, the computer found its way to Line 40 and a condition that was true. (Yes, 12 is less than 13.) The feedback ("Try a larger number.") was **PRINT**ed and the computer dutifully looped back to Line 10 and asked the question once again.

The third time through, we were intoxicated with confidence. We were sure we had the right answer. So, bold as you please, we typed in 13. The computer tucked it in **ANSWER** and went with it to Line 30 and Line 40, discovering that the conditions were false on both lines. Finally, it was able to make its way to line 50, where it **PRINT**ed out its congratulatory message. Only then was the noble beast willing to take its well-deserved rest.

SUMMARY

Conditional statements teach the computer how to *analyze* information that users enter in **INPUT** statements. This type of analysis, either with string or numeric variables, is extremely useful when writing interactive programs. In the minds of the uninitiated, it creates the impression of computer intelligence and a look of "how did it do that?" To the initiated, whose ranks you have just joined, there is no mystery—it's just a matter of **IF** and **THEN**.

6 QUIZ

1. When you use a statement that begins with **IF**, don't forget the:
    a. mustard
    b. **THAN**
    c. **THEN**

2. Which of the following lines contains a syntax error?

```
10 IF ANSWER$ = "computer" THEN PRINT "An excellent
   choice."
20 IF ANSWER$ = 1750 THEN PRINT "That sounds like it's
   too high."
30 IF ANSWER$ = "ELEPHANT" THEN GOTO 100
```

3. In most BASICs, it's all right to add a command to the end of a conditional statement as long as the command is preceded by a:
    a. semicolon
    b. colon
    c. line number

4. When you use **OR** in a conditional statement, how many of the conditions must be true before the computer will execute the command?

    a. one of them
    b. one more than half of them
    c. all of them

5. Which of the following is not a use of **IF/THEN**?

    a. deal with unexpected input
    b. impress the computer
    c. compare values

6. The "less than" symbol looks like an arrow pointing to the right. True or False?

7. Which of the following symbols (when not inside quotes) can be contained in an **IF/THEN** statement?

    a. $<$
    b. !
    c. $>$
    d. $=$
    e. $<>$

7 FOR/NEXT

Controlled loops: Do it for a while then stop!

As we saw in Chapter 5 and again in Chapter 6, the use of the **GOTO** command really makes things easier for programmer and user alike. The **GOTO** loop is invaluable when used in an **IF/THEN** statement like this one:

```
30 IF NAME$ = "TANYA" THEN GOTO 50
```

The statement on Line 30 is known as a *conditional loop* since the **GOTO** command will only be executed if the condition is true. As we saw in Chapter 5, a **GOTO** statement can also be used *without* being preceded by a conditional statement. There we presented an unconditional **GOTO** after an **INPUT** statement, as we've done in the following program:

```
NEW

10 PRINT "Who is going to win the World Series?";
20 INPUT TEAM$
30 PRINT "How can you say ";TEAM$;"?"
40 GOTO 10
```

When we **RUN** this program, we get

```
RUN

Who is going to win the World Series? Yankees
How can you say Yankees?
Who is going to win the World Series? Dodgers
How can you say Dodgers?
Who is going to win the World Series? Red Sox
How can you say Red Sox?
Who is going to win the World Series?

BREAK IN LINE 20
```

The program will continue in this manner until we press the interrupt key and let the computer know we've had enough! Because the **INPUT** statement always waits while the user is answering the question, the new loop will not begin until the answer has been received. Although this is a runaway loop

(which, if left to its own devices, will go on forever), the user will not have the same experience of utter craziness as he or she will have with the following non-interactive program.

```
NEW

10 PRINT "How do you stop this thing?"
20 GOTO 10
```

Are you ready for this? Just watch what happens when we **RUN** this simple two-line program.

```
RUN

How do you stop this thing?
How do you stop this thing?
How do you stop this thing?
How do you stop this thing?
How do you stop this thing?
How do you stop this thing?
How do you stop this thing?
How do you stop this thing?
How do you stop this thing?
How do you stop this thing?

BREAK IN LINE 10
```

In a fraction of a second, the screen is filled to overflowing with "How do you stop this thing?" and it doesn't stop there. The computer will continue to **PRINT** until someone turns the machine off or presses the interrupt key (as we did). This, too, is a runaway loop and, because it is totally uncontrollable from within the program, it is simply not a very effective technique.

GETTING IT UNDER CONTROL

Suppose we want the computer to do something *more than once* but less than forever. What command could we use in a case like that? BASIC does provide programmers with a more refined and civilized loop called **FOR/NEXT**, and it is perfect for such occasions. Allow us to explain.

BASIC's **FOR/NEXT** loops are *counting loops*. When you use them, your computer will perform a task only a *certain number of times*. Since you specify the number, you will never have to worry about the manic behavior of a runaway loop because you always know when the computer will stop.

All **FOR/NEXT** loops are paired statements.* If one of the words is present in a program, the other must be there too. The words **FOR** and **NEXT** go together like a cup and saucer and you cannot have one without the other. Here's an example of a program containing a **FOR/NEXT** loop.

```
NEW

10 FOR ECHO = 1 TO 5
20 PRINT "Hello there!"
30 NEXT ECHO
```

The loop in this program begins on Line 10 (with the words **FOR ECHO**) and ends on Line 30 (with the words **NEXT ECHO**).

We know that this program looks totally unfamiliar, but so did **PRINT** when you first saw it. Let's try **RUN**ning it and see what it does.

```
RUN

Hello there!
Hello there!
Hello there!
Hello there!
Hello there!
```

---

*Another example of a paired statement is **IF/THEN**.

Isn't that interesting? The computer **PRINT**ed our string five times. Let's pick the program apart now and see how it works.

Line 10 is the proper way to start a **FOR/NEXT** loop, that is, with a line number (of course) and the word **FOR**. What *always* follows the word **FOR** is a *numeric variable* because, as we mentioned earlier, a **FOR/NEXT** loop is a *counting* loop.

After the numeric variable **ECHO** comes an equal sign (=) followed by one number, the word **TO**, and finally another number. Translated into English, Line 10 means *begin a counting loop, placing the numbers 1 to 5, one at a time, in the variable called ECHO.*

In other words, imagine that we've asked the computer to drop a number into a box labeled **ECHO**. Because the box is so small, it will only be able to hold one number at a time. As soon as the second number is tossed in, the first number will automatically be tossed out, and so on. The purpose of Line 10 is to keep track of the number of times a task (Line 20) is to be done.

Line 20 tells the computer to **PRINT** the string "Hello there!" The number 5 in Line 10 tells the computer this command is going to be executed five times, and it was. The number 5 is referred to as the *final value* of the loop, while the number 1 is called the *initial value*.

Line 30 is the loop (or "return again") part of the **FOR/NEXT** loop. When the computer sees this line, it hears the following message: *Increment (increase) ECHO, and go back to the FOR ECHO line* (Line 10).

When the computer returns to Line 10, it checks to see if the value in **ECHO** is less than or equal to 5. If the value is less than 5, the computer will go through the loop again, this time putting into **ECHO** the next number in the sequence.

If the value is greater than 5, the computer will drop down to the line *after* **NEXT ECHO** (if there is one). In this case, **NEXT ECHO** (Line 30) *is* the last line in the program; so when the value is more than 5, the program will end.

Teaching the Computer to Count Out Loud

In the last program, the computer was putting the numbers from 1 to 5 in the loop's variable (**ECHO**). We know that it was putting the numbers there because our command to **PRINT** "Hello there!" was executed five times.

We never did see those numbers on the screen, however. This time we are going to create a **FOR/NEXT** loop whose task will be to **PRINT** the contents of the loop's variable. Here's the program.

```
10 FOR TURN = 5 TO 10
20 PRINT TURN
30 NEXT TURN
```

Now let's **RUN** the program and see it count.

```
RUN

5
6
7
8
9
10
```

Wait a moment. It counted from 5 to 10. Well, if we look at Line 10, we'll see that this is exactly what we told it to do. The initial value was 5 and the final value was 10. The numbers from 5 to 10 were placed in the loop's variable **TURN**, and then Line 20 **PRINT**ed them on the screen.

Now that we understand how the **FOR/NEXT** loop operates, let's really put it to work.

Write That 20 Times

Remember the time you were caught chewing gum in History class? Well, with the help of a computer and a **FOR/NEXT** loop, creating the following punishment assignment would be a snap.

```
NEW

10 FOR CHEW = 1 TO 20
20 PRINT CHEW;" I will not chew gum in class."
30 NEXT CHEW
```

This program begins on Line 10 with a **FOR/NEXT** loop that is going to fill the variable **CHEW** with numbers from 1 to 20. In addition to telling the machine to **PRINT** the contents of **CHEW** (as was done with **PRINT TURN** on Line 20 of the previous program), Line 20 tells the machine to **PRINT** the string, "I will not chew gum in class."

Line 30 is the end of the **FOR/NEXT** loop. It tells the computer to go back to the line of the program that starts with the words **FOR CHEW** and put the next number in the box.

When we **RUN** this program, we get a speedily **PRINT**ed result that would surely impress even the staunchest of anti-gum disciplinarians.

```
RUN

 1 I will not chew gum in class.
 2 I will not chew gum in class.
 3 I will not chew gum in class.
 4 I will not chew gum in class.
 5 I will not chew gum in class.
 6 I will not chew gum in class.
 7 I will not chew gum in class.
 8 I will not chew gum in class.
 9 I will not chew gum in class.
10 I will not chew gum in class.
11 I will not chew gum in class.
12 I will not chew gum in class.
13 I will not chew gum in class.
14 I will not chew gum in class.
15 I will not chew gum in class.
16 I will not chew gum in class.
17 I will not chew gum in class.
18 I will not chew gum in class.
19 I will not chew gum in class.
20 I will not chew gum in class.
```

Racers, Take Your Mark

Now to dazzle you even more, let's write a program that PRINTs the actual numbers being stored in the variable right in the middle of a string. The program we've created for this astounding demonstration displays five identical race cars poised at the starting line.

No, we're not about to start teaching the kind of fancy programming that is seen on the video arcade games. We just want to give you a better idea of what a FOR/NEXT loop can do. Here is the program.

```
NEW

10 PRINT "Welcome to Computer Race Day!"
20 PRINT
30 FOR CAR = 1 TO 5
40 PRINT "       ‾‾‾‾‾    "
50 PRINT "/‾‾‾‾‾\ ___ "
60 PRINT "I      ";CAR;"    I"
70 PRINT "-(o)---(o)-"
80 NEXT CAR
90 PRINT "And they're off!"
```

In this program the **FOR/NEXT** loop starts on Line 30 and ends on Line 80. (Line 90 will be executed when the loop is completed.) Don't be thrown by Lines 40, 50, 60, and 70. They are **PRINT** statements and everything in them contained within quotation marks (including blank spaces) will be displayed on the screen, character for character.

What is *not* contained within quotes is the variable **CAR** as well as the semicolons that surround it. This will cause the computer to **PRINT** the contents of **CAR**, that is, the numbers from 1 to 5.

Now, let's **RUN** the program and see what we've got in the line-up today.

```
RUN

Welcome to Computer Race Day!
  /-----\---
  |    1    |
  -(o)---(o)-


  /-----\---
  |    2    |
  -(o)---(o)-


  /-----\---
  |    3    |
  -(o)---(o)-


  /-----\---
  |    4    |
  -(o)---(o)-


  /-----\---
  |    5    |
  -(o)---(o)-
And they're off!
```

The computer did most of the work. We typed in the characters that made up one race car and the computer made five perfect, numbered copies.

We'll Give You Just Three Guesses

We hope your mind is just going wild with the possibilities that make themselves apparent now that you know the computer has this capability. With the control afforded to you by the **FOR/NEXT** loop, you can use any BASIC command and get the computer to do any task any number of times.

For example, suppose you want the computer to create a math problem (see the $6 + 7 = ?$ program from Chapter 6) but, instead of giving the student an unlimited number of chances to get the right answer, this time we're only going to give him or her three chances.

Using a combination of **IF/THEN** and **FOR/NEXT**, we're going to have the program give some feedback and repeat the problem until the third try. If student has not succeeded after three guesses, then we're going to tell him or her what the right answer is. Here's the program.

```
NEW

10 FOR GUESS = 1 TO 3
20 PRINT "What is the product of 12 * 5";
30 INPUT ANSWER
40 IF ANSWER < 60 THEN PRINT ANSWER;" is too low.":
   GOTO 70
50 IF ANSWER > 60 THEN PRINT ANSWER;" is too high.":
   GOTO 70
60 PRINT "Correct. It took ";GUESS;" guess(es).":GOTO 90
70 NEXT GUESS
80 PRINT "Sorry, it's 60."
90 END
```

This is the most complicated program we've done so far, but we're sure you will understand it in a minute. As always, we'll just look at it line by line and see how it works.

Line 10 is the beginning of our **FOR/NEXT** loop. It tells the computer that we want it to put the numbers 1 to 3 in succession into a variable called **GUESS**. Line 20 **PRINT**s the string "What is the product of 12 * 5." Line 30 accepts an answer and stores it in the numeric variable called **ANSWER**. That means we have two variables in this program.

The one called **GUESS** keeps track of the number of guesses and the one called **ANSWER** stores the user's answer to the question. This is a perfect example of why the use of nondescriptive variables like **X** and **Y** can be confusing.

Line 40 checks if the number in **ANSWER** is less than 60. If it is, the computer **PRINT**s that number (whatever it is) along with the string "is too low." *and* goes to Line 70 to increment **GUESS** and begin the next loop.

Line 50 is similar; it checks if the number in **ANSWER** is more than 60. If it is, the computer **PRINT**s that number (whatever it is) along with the string "is too high." *and* goes to Line 70, as before.

If the computer ever gets to Line 60, then the answer must be correct; therefore, an **IF/THEN** in front of the **PRINT** is not necessary. When the answer is correct, the computer will automatically **PRINT** out, "Correct. It took (however many guesses it took guess (es))."

If the computer loops through the program three times without receiving a correct answer, the computer will exit the **FOR/NEXT** loop and will drop down to Line 80 and **PRINT**, "Sorry, it's 60."

Line 90 contains a new statement, **END**. All this statement does is tell the computer that the program has ended.

That's the explanation. Now let's see what it looks like.

```
RUN

What is the product of 12 * 5? 60
Correct. It took 1 guess(es).
```

Congratulations! Now this time let's see what happens when we are not so quick with our multiplication facts.

```
RUN

What is the product of 12 * 5? 17
17 is too low.
What is the product of 12 * 5? 72
72 is too high.
What is the product of 12 * 5? 60
Correct. It took 3 guess(es).
```

Three guesses, and we got in just under the wire. Let's try it one more time and see what happens if we miss it completely.

```
RUN

What is the product of 12 * 5? 84
84 is too high.
What is the product of 12 * 5? 83
83 is too high.
What is the product of 12 * 5? 59
59 is too low.
Sorry, it's 60.
```

Oh well, maybe we'll do better next time. Anyway, we now have a clear understanding of the standard way of using **FOR/NEXT** loops. Before we go on to other things, though, you should be aware of the variations that are possible when using **FOR/NEXT**.

VARIATIONS

As we just mentioned, there are other ways of implementing a **FOR/NEXT** loop. Here are three of them.

Creating a Pause

As we explained when we first introduced **FOR/NEXT** at the beginning of this chapter, the loop causes numbers to be placed in sequence into a variable. Some of the programs we showed earlier in this chapter **PRINT**ed the current value of the variable on the screen, and so we saw the numbers.

The computer, however, will place the numbers in the variable even if we *don't* tell it to **PRINT**. This kind of *invisible counting* is the way pauses can be created in programs. Look, for example, at the following simple program:

```
NEW

10 PRINT "Take a deep breath."
20 FOR GASP = 1 TO 1000
30 NEXT GASP
40 PRINT "Now exhale."
```

When we **RUN** this program, the computer will pause for a few seconds between **PRINT**ing "Take a deep breath." and "Now exhale." The precise amount of time will vary depending on the computer, but it will usually not take more than a few seconds for the computer to count internally from 1 to 1000! (Since there is no command that tells the computer to **PRINT GASP**, the actual numbers 1 to 1000 will not be displayed.) The pause can always be lengthened or shortened by changing the final value of the counting loop.

So remember this in the course of your programming career. If you ever want to create a pause during the execution of a program so that the computer displays something on the screen and leaves it there for a while before it displays something else, you can do it with a **FOR/NEXT** loop.

Varying the Start and Stop Numbers

The initial and final values of a **FOR/NEXT** loop need not be preset by the programmer. They can be entered (via an **INPUT** statement) by the user. For example, you could write a program that asks the user which numbers he or she would like to have as the beginning and end of the loop. You would start as follows:

```
NEW

10 PRINT "I am going to count for you."
20 PRINT "Where would you like me to start";
30 INPUT START
40 PRINT "And where should I stop";
50 INPUT FINI
60 PRINT
70 FOR NUMBER = START TO FINI
80 PRINT NUMBER
90 NEXT NUMBER
100 PRINT "All done."
```

Let's **RUN** the program and see what happens.

```
RUN

I am going to count for you.
Where would you like me to start? 13
And where should I stop? 21

13
14
15
16
17
18
19
20
21
All done.
```

In this program, the numbers from **START** to **FINI** are stored in **NUMBER** and **PRINT**ed in succession on the screen.

Watch Me Count by Twos

In every program in this chapter we have shown the computer's ability to count, or increment, by 1. Incrementing a **FOR/NEXT** command by a value other than 1 is achieved with the optional control **STEP**. It literally tells the computer that the **STEP** you want it to take from one number to the next is going to be something greater than or less than 1. For example, if you want the computer to count from 6 to 12 by 2, you would write your **FOR/NEXT** loop like this.

```
NEW

10 FOR NUMBER = 6 TO 12 STEP 2
20 PRINT NUMBER
30 NEXT NUMBER
```

The **RUN** would look like the following:

```
RUN

6
8
10
12
```

To get the computer to count backwards, write your loop as shown on the following screen.

```
NEW

10 FOR NUMBER = 116 TO 97 STEP -5
20 PRINT NUMBER
30 NEXT NUMBER
```

When we **RUN** this one, we get

```
RUN

116
111
106
101
```

As you can see, the computer never got to 97 because by subtracting 5 from 101 it would have come up with 96. In a case like this, the computer will always decrement or increment according to command for as long as it can *without going past* the ending number of the **FOR/NEXT** loop.

There you have it: the inner workings of a very powerful and versatile BASIC command. The **FOR/NEXT** loop can be used in many different ways, and we'll see it again in Chapter 8 when we start playing around with random numbers.

SUMMARY

The computer uses **FOR/NEXT** loops to keep track of how many times a certain task is to be executed. The command offers the convenience of a copying machine. It makes a programmer's job easier because of its ability to work over the same instructions as many times as desired without the necessity of rewriting the instructions each time. Programming without **FOR/NEXT** (when applicable) is like trying to shovel snow with a spoon—it can be done, but it certainly takes longer.

7 QUIZ

1. A **FOR/NEXT** loop can be used to tell the computer to:
   - *a.* multiply two numbers
   - *b.* continue repeating several lines of instructions indefinitely
   - *c.* repeat several lines of instructions a prescribed number of times

2. What (if anything) is wrong with this **FOR/NEXT** loop?

```
10 NEXT LOOP
20 PRINT "Here is a counting loop."
30 FOR LOOP = 1 TO 10
```

3. The **FOR** command and the **NEXT** command can occupy two separate lines: True or False?

4. Which line of the following program contains a syntax error:

```
10 FOR ZEBRA = 1 TO 8
20 PRINT "This is zebra number ";ZEBRA
30 ANOTHER ZEBRA
```

5. If you wanted to change this program to print "Hello" seven times, which line would have to be rewritten?

```
10 FOR LOOP = 1 TO 5
20 PRINT "Hello"
30 NEXT LOOP
```

153

6. A **FOR/NEXT** loop can start with which of the following (only one answer is correct)?

   a. `FOR LOOP$ = 1 TO 15`
   b. `FOR LOOPS = 6 TO 12`
   c. `FOR LOOP = 3 - 99`

8 RANDOM NUMBERS

Where it stops, nobody knows

Playing around with random events brings out the gambler in each of us. Whether it's guessing what number will be picked, where something will land, or whether a flipped coin will turn up heads, it's all equally fascinating. When working with computers and random numbers, the programming process is relatively simple.

In addition, because the results are available almost instantly, the amazing speed and power of the machine are revealed. As we will soon see, randomizing events provides some intriguing programming possibilities. In this chapter we will be using what we've learned in conjunction with a new command to create some random number programs.

PICK A RANDOM NUMBER

The first step in turning the computer into a Wheel of Fortune is to teach it how to choose a random number. As we mentioned above, the programming process is not difficult. Essentially, it consists of a single line of instruction called the *random number formula.* Here it is.

```
10 LET RNUMBER = INT(RND(1) * 10 + 1)
```

155

What a conglomeration of parentheses! And what are **INT** and **RND**? The whole thing looks pretty horrendous, doesn't it? That was the same reaction *we* had the first time we saw it, but actually it's not that bad. If we take this formula and translate it into our native tongue, we will see that it can be easily understood. The following statement tells us what it all means: *Create a numeric variable and call it* **RNUMBER**. *Put in that variable a whole number chosen randomly from any one of the numbers from 1 to 10.*

If, for example, you want the computer to choose a number from 1 to 100, you could do it by programming the following line:

```
20 LET CHOOSE = INT(RND(1) * 100 + 1)
```

The major difference between Line 20 and Line 10 is that instead of multiplying

```
RND(1)*10
```

we are now multiplying

```
RND(1)*100
```

When the multiplier is 10, the computer picks a number from 1 to 10. When the multiplier is 100, the computer chooses a number from 1 to 100. It's that simple.

As you probably also noticed, we changed the name of the numeric variable from **RNUMBER** to **CHOOSE**. We did this to remind you that the name of a variable can be changed at will. The only rule to follow is that, in the random number formula, the variable must be a *numeric variable*. The actual name of the variable itself can be anything.

What the RANDOM NUMBER Formula Really Means

If you are the type of person who is not entirely satisfied with our English translation of the Random Number Formula, we are going to offer you more. For you, we will dissect each parenthesis and reveal the inner workings of this mathematical statement. If you would rather use the formula on faith without delving deeper, then just skip this next section and go on to "Cranking Up the Random Number Generator."

Programmed into the computer as a part of BASIC is a never ending series of nonrepeating decimals *between* 0 and 1 (that is, *never* 0 and *never* 1, but anything in between). This number series is the basis of all computer generated "random" numbers. Because these numbers are part of a *series* and not truly random, they are called "pseudo" random numbers.

You can access these random numbers with the **RND(1)*** function. For example, if you type

```
NEW

10 PRINT RND(1)
20 GOTO 10
```

when you **RUN**, you will get numbers similar to the following:

```
RUN

0.568572
0.243606
0.499038
0.898483
0.461898
0.923507

BREAK IN LINE 10
```

As you can see, these numbers are all decimals that are less than 1. What would you do if you wanted the computer to generate numbers between 0 and 100?

In BASIC, the instructions would appear as

```
NEW

10 PRINT RND(1) * 100
20 GOTO 10
```

---

*In some versions of BASIC, the number inside the parentheses is meaningless. In others, it must be a 0 (zero). And in some versions, the random function (RND) will return a whole number from 1 to the number within the parentheses.

When you **RUN** it this time, the numbers look like this.

```
RUN

22.7416
63.0401
80.2932
26.6159
51.4724


BREAK IN LINE 10
```

Now if we didn't want to deal with decimals, we would need to rewrite Line 10 of the above program so that it looks like this.

```
10 PRINT INT(RND(1) * 100)
```

Line 10 includes one set of parentheses inside of another. These are called *nested parentheses*. The rule about them is that the computer will always work with the innermost set first and then proceed to the outermost set.

The innermost set of parentheses contains

```
RND(1) * 100
```

This tells the computer to choose a random number between 0 and 100, complete with decimals, as we just saw in the last program. The outermost set of parentheses is guarded by INT (which stands for INTeger, or *whole number*).

Whenever the computer sees the INT command, it takes the value within INT's parentheses, strips away any numbers to the right of the decimal point, and comes up with a number which is the next lower whole number value.

If this Line 10 had been part of the program during the preceding RUN, the resulting numbers would have been

```
22
63
80
26
51
```

The only problem with what we have now is that it will only yield the numbers *from* 0 to 99. So if we have our hearts set on getting access to all the numbers from 1 to 100, we have to add 1 (+1) to our formula. Here's what we have got now.

```
10 LET R = INT(RND(1) * 100 + 1)
```

Suppose the computer receives this command and returns the number 0.682431 from its built-in number series. According to the instructions of the formula, the computer would multiply 0.682431 by 100 and get 68.2431. Next the formula says "add one" (+1) so that 68.2431 becomes 69.2431. And finally, because INT means "make a whole number" to the computer, 69.2431 becomes 69, which is, in fact, a random number within our range of 1 to 100.

It should be noted that since some computers always start at the same point in the series of nonrepeating decimals when they are first turned on, the random numbers that are generated may in fact be very predictable.

CRANKING UP THE RANDOM NUMBER GENERATOR

Now that we know what the formula does, let's write a short program and watch it work. We'll start out with an important sounding title to be prominently displayed, highlighted with asterisks, and followed by a blank line. Here's what it looks like so far.

```
NEW

10 PRINT "*** A Random Number Generator ***"
20 PRINT
```

Since this program is going to generate random numbers, we need the random number formula. And while we're at it, let's set it up to tell the computer to select a random number from 1 to 100.

```
30 LET SELECT = INT(RND(1) * 100 + 1)
```

As it would be useful to have the computer *display* the selected number on the screen, we also need to have a **PRINT** command in the program. The following one will do nicely:

```
40 PRINT SELECT
```

Finally, we would like the computer to return to Lines 30 and 40 and repeat eight times the entire process of choosing a number and displaying it on the screen. As we learned in Chapter 7, this is a job for a **FOR/NEXT** loop!

One small problem: Where does the **FOR** go and where does the **NEXT** go? (Remember, *everything* that is sandwiched in between the **FOR** command and the **NEXT** command is going to be repeated the prescribed number of times.)

To figure out where the loop starts and ends, we have to decide which is the first line of instruction we are going to want the computer to repeat. How about the **PRINT** statement on Line 10? That's our title. Do we want to have it **PRINT**ed eight times? Not really. Therefore, it does not need to be *within* the loop. The same goes for the blank line that's going to be **PRINT**ed after the title as a result of Line 20.

Since we want the computer to select eight random numbers and **PRINT** each of them, the machine is going to have to visit Lines 30 and 40 eight times. Therefore, Lines 30 and 40 are the only two lines that should be *within* the loop. The **FOR** command must begin *before Line 30* (Line 25 would be a good place).

```
25 FOR LOOP = 1 TO 8
```

Also, the **NEXT** command must be placed *after Line 40* (we can put it on Line 50).

```
50 NEXT LOOP
```

Now follows an example of the whole program, including the **FOR/NEXT** loop and the lines within it.

```
LIST

10 PRINT "*** A Random Number Generator ***"
20 PRINT
25 FOR LOOP = 1 TO 8
30 LET SELECT = INT(RND(1) * 100 + 1)
40 PRINT SELECT
50 NEXT LOOP
```

We're now ready to **RUN** and watch the magic of the random number generator. As we will see, because of the nature of the random number formula, each number between 1 and 100 has an equal chance of being selected.

```
RUN

*** A Random Number Generator ***

72
2
33
96
100
8
47
47
```

There you have it. Eight randomly selected numbers. Notice that the computer chose the number 47 two times in succession. This shows that the random number formula is *not* the same as the random selection of, for example, a Bingo ball from a revolving cage. Although both are random processes, when N47 is selected in Bingo, it is taken out of circulation and cannot be chosen at any other time during the game.

Let's RUN this program again and see which eight numbers come up this time.

```
RUN

86
43
61
82
38
56
14
1
```

It looks like another completely random selection. It's great fun when the computer comes up with totally unexpected results (as long as you program it to do that).

Okay, now let's do something else with random numbers. Suppose we want the computer to look for a specific number and to keep looking until it is found. How would we put something like that together in BASIC?

Keep on Picking

Rather than just having some numbers displayed on the screen, it would be a good idea to begin the program by displaying an explanation of what's happening. We can do that with the following two **PRINT** statements:

```
NEW

10 PRINT "I am randomly picking numbers between 1 and
   12."
20 PRINT "I will stop when I find the number 8."
```

Now, to separate the explanation from the actual choice of numbers, let's program the computer to **PRINT** a blank line on the screen.

```
30 PRINT
```

For the important part of the program, we need a line with a random number formula (this time we're going to use the numeric variable **R**). And for a change of pace, instead of having the computer choose a number from 1 to 100, let's have it choose a number between 1 and 12.

```
40 LET R = INT(RND(1) * 12 + 1)
```

In this program, as in the one before, we would also like the computer to **PRINT** out the number that it selects, and so we need a **PRINT** command and we can put it on Line 50.

```
50 PRINT R
```

Now just for a little variation and excitement, suppose we have the computer keep on picking random numbers until it specifically finds the number 8. In that case, we're not going to be able to use the services of a

FOR/NEXT loop because we are not telling the computer to do a task *a specified number of times*. Instead, we're telling the computer to do the task *as many times as it needs to* until the number is found.

Is there a BASIC command that can fit the bill? Ah yes, a conditional **GOTO** statement. An **IF/THEN** statement with a **GOTO** at the end, a command we first learned about in Chapter 6, is the very thing we need. The line will look like this.

```
60 IF R <> 8 THEN GOTO 40
```

This instruction tells the computer if the random number that was chosen (on Line 40) and stored in variable **R** is *not equal* to 8, then it is to go back to Line 40 and choose a new random number.

The computer will keep returning to Line 40 until the condition on Line 60 is no longer true. When will **R** not be *not equal* to 8? When **R** *is equal* to 8, of course! When this happens, the computer will drop down to the next line, which states

```
70 PRINT "Eureka! I found the number 8!"
```

Please notice that Line 70 does not contain a conditional statement declaring

```
IF R = 8 THEN PRINT "Eureka!"
```

Line 70 wouldn't be wrong if you programmed it like that. But it's not necessary since the computer will only be reading the instructions on Line 70 when R equals 8. Therefore, the condition is implied and doesn't need to be stated.

Now we can **LIST** the program and look it over in its entirety.

```
LIST

10 PRINT "I am randomly picking numbers between 1 and
   12."
20 PRINT "I will stop when I find the number 8."
30 PRINT
40 LET R = INT(RND(1) * 12 + 1)
50 PRINT R
60 IF R <> 8 THEN GOTO 40
70 PRINT "Eureka! I found the number 8!"
```

Now we're ready to spin the wheel and see how long the computer takes to select the lucky number 8.

```
RUN

I am randomly picking numbers between 1 and 12.
I will stop when I find the number 8.

3
11
6
8
Eureka! I found the number 8!
```

How about that? The computer picked the number 8 in four tries. Let's RUN the program again and see how it does this time.

```
RUN

I am randomly picking numbers between 1 and 12.
I will stop when I find the number 8.

2
8
Eureka! I found the number 8!
```

Wow, that time it took only two tries for the computer to come up with our lucky number! We must be on a roll. Let's take everything we've "won" so far and put it all on the next RUN.

```
RUN

I am randomly picking numbers between 1 and 12.
I will stop when I find the number 8.

12
10
12
6
2
9
10
10
3
1
9
8
Eureka! I found the number 8!
```

Oh well, the Fickle Finger of Fate strikes again. It took the computer 12 times to find the number 8 and we ended up losing our entire bankroll. Sigh!

Select Your Own Lucky Number

We think that this program, mildly entertaining though it is, would be even more fun if we allowed the user to choose his or her own lucky number. (That way there would be a greater feeling of control over the outcome.)

To modify the program so that it is interactive and the user can tell the computer which number to search for (as opposed to that information being designated by the programmer), we need an **INPUT** statement.

How about a program that starts off with

```
NEW

10 PRINT "I can find the number of your choice."
20 PRINT "What is your favorite number between 1 and
   12";
30 INPUT NUMBER
32 PRINT
```

Now, instead of telling the computer to choose a new random number until the number 8 is found, we're going to tell it to keep choosing numbers until the user's lucky number (whatever it is) is found.

The rest of the program would look like this.

```
40 LET R = INT(RND(1) * 12 + 1)
50 PRINT R
60 IF R <> NUMBER THEN GOTO 40
70 PRINT "Eureka! I found the number ";NUMBER;"!"
```

As you can see, the major difference between this program and the one we just ran is Line 60. Line 60 of the previous program stated

```
IF R <> 8 THEN GOTO 40
```

Line 60 of this new program tells the machine

```
IF R <> NUMBER THEN GOTO 40
```

In other words, it tells the computer, "If the random number you choose is not equal to the user's lucky number, then return to Line 40 and choose a new number."

Line 70 of the new program is similar to Line 70 of the previous program, but instead of **PRINT**ing the fact that it found the number 8, the computer will **PRINT** that it found the user's lucky number.

Now we're ready to try out the program.

```
RUN

I can find the number of your choice.
What is your favorite number between 1 and 12? 5


3
6
2
2
7
5
Eureka! I found the number 5!
```

It seems to be working just fine. But it could be better. Do you remember that we talked in Chapter 6 about what to do when the computer is programmed to answer questions with "yes" and "no" and the user INPUTs a "maybe"? It would certainly mess up the program if the programmer hadn't been prepared for that possibility.

We would have the same problem with this random number program should the user stick in a lucky number that is *more than* 12. How can anyone expect a computer to find a number more than 12 if it's only going to select numbers from 1 to 12?

It can't be done. But the simple-minded computer would just keep returning to Line 40 until they carted it away to the chip factory.

To prepare for the potentially uncooperative user, we need to program a line like the following:

```
34 IF NUMBER > 12 THEN PRINT "I'm not picking numbers
   higher than 12.": GOTO 20
```

With a line like this we can tell the computer what to do if the number it receives is greater than 12. Line 34 tells the machine to inform the user, "I'm not picking numbers higher than 12" and return to Line 20 where the question, "What is your favorite number between 1 and 12?" is asked again.

Let's **LIST** the program now.

```
LIST

10 PRINT "I can find your favorite number."
20 PRINT "What is your favorite number between 1 and
   12";
30 INPUT NUMBER
32 PRINT
34 IF NUMBER > 12 THEN PRINT "I'm not picking numbers
   higher than 12.": GOTO 20
40 LET R = INT(RND(1) * 12 + 1)
50 PRINT R
60 IF R <> NUMBER THEN GOTO 40
70 PRINT "Eureka! I found the number ";NUMBER;"!"
```

Now watch how the program handles an inappropriate response.

```
RUN

I can find the number of your choice.
What is your favorite number between 1 and 12? 14

I'm not picking numbers higher than 12.
What is your favorite number between 1 and 12? 0.5


4
12
7
2
11
9
6

BREAK IN LINE 40
```

Uh, oh. Another problem. And just when we were doing so well. What's going on here is that the computer is racing down another wrong track. It is hopelessly lost in its search for the number 0.5, which of course it's never going to find among the numbers between 1 and 12.

Never fear, the **IF/THEN** statement is here. We can take care of the numbers that are less than 1 in the same manner that we handled the numbers that are more than 12.

```
36 IF NUMBER < 1 THEN PRINT "I'm not picking numbers
   lower than 1.": GOTO 20
```

This time we are instructing the computer to see if the number it receives is less than 1 and, if it is, to **PRINT** the message, "I'm not picking numbers lower than 1." At that point, the computer will return to Line 20 and the user will be given another opportunity to **INPUT** a number.

With the addition of Lines 34 and 36, we can feel confident. When we **RUN** the following program, we just know we're prepared for everybody, even people who cannot or will not follow directions:

```
LIST

10 PRINT "I can find your favorite number."
20 PRINT "What is your favorite number between 1 and
   12";
30 INPUT NUMBER
32 PRINT
34 IF NUMBER > 12 THEN PRINT "I'm not picking numbers
   higher than 12.": GOTO 20
36 IF NUMBER < 1 THEN PRINT "I'm not picking numbers
   lower than 1.": GOTO 20
40 LET R = INT(RND(1) * 12 + 1)
50 PRINT R
60 IF R <> NUMBER THEN GOTO 40
70 PRINT "Eureka! I found the number ";NUMBER;"!"
```

Now let's **RUN** it.

```
RUN

I can find the number of your choice.
What is your favorite number between 1 and 12? 19

I'm not picking numbers higher than 12.
What is your favorite number between 1 and 12? -4

I'm not picking numbers lower than 1.
What is your favorite number between 1 and 12? 3.2

5
9
1
1
4
8
3
BREAK IN 40
```

Stop everything! Did you see that? These machines certainly aren't very bright. The user put in 3.2 and the computer is off and running, trying to find it.

So that's one more possibility we neglected. What happens when the user **INPUT**s a number that is between 1 and 12 but that is *not* a whole number? To take care of that kind of situation, we need a line that tells the computer to accept only integers (whole numbers).

The **INT** command, which we saw earlier in our random number formula and which means "whole number, disregarding any decimals," would work here. A line enabling our program to take care of numbers like 3.2 would resemble

```
38 IF NUMBER <> INT(NUMBER) THEN PRINT "Please stick to
   whole numbers.":GOTO 20
```

This line means: *If NUMBER (in this case, 3.2) is not equal to the INTeger of NUMBER (3) then PRINT "Please stick to whole numbers" and return to Line 20 and request a new number.*

Let's **LIST** this program now, see what the whole thing looks like, and then give it the acid test.

```
LIST

10 PRINT "I can find the number of your choice."
20 PRINT "What is your favorite number between 1 and
   12";
30 INPUT NUMBER
32 PRINT
34 IF NUMBER > 12 THEN PRINT "I'm not picking numbers
   higher than 12.": GOTO 20
36 IF NUMBER < 1 THEN PRINT "I'm not picking numbers
   lower than 1.": GOTO 20
38 IF NUMBER <> INT(NUMBER) THEN PRINT "Please stick to
   whole numbers.":GOTO 20
40 LET R = INT(RND(1) * 12 + 1)
50 PRINT R
60 IF R <> NUMBER THEN GOTO 40
70 PRINT "Eureka! I found the number ";NUMBER;"!"
```

It seems a bit complex. But since we've gone through each part of it line by line, it should all look familiar to you at this point.

We can now **RUN** this program with a real sense of security because, even if the user manages to misread the directions and **INPUT**s a number that is larger than 12 or smaller than 1 or enters a mixed number (like 7.592), our computer is prepared.

```
RUN

I can find your favorite number.
What is your favorite number between 1 and 12? 9.99

Please stick to whole numbers.
What is your favorite number between 1 and 12? 12.004

I'm not picking numbers higher than 12.
What is your favorite number between 1 and 12? 7

4
8
11
9
4
3
4
7
Eureka! I found the number 7!
```

Oh happy day! We're finished with this program and our lesson on random numbers. And although we did not, by any means, cover the full potential that can evolve from the use of random numbers, we hope you have enough information now to start imagining some of the other possibilities. (In case you would like a hint, other uses of random numbers in programming include randomizing acknowledgments in computerized quizzes and randomizing player choices and outcomes in adventure games.)

SUMMARY

Random numbers are used most often in BASIC programs to add unpredictability to simulations when programming gambling-type games and random events. The random number formula provides the programmer with the ability to create surprises for the user, and this adds to the seemingly magical properties of the computer.

8 QUIZ

1. When you tell a computer to "pick a random number from 1 to 10," you can use this formula:

   a. E = MC2
   b. R = INT(RND(1) * 10 + 1)
   c. A = L * W
   d. GOLD = TOADSKINS + PEANUTBUTTER

2. Which of the following can be simulated using the random number formula?

   a. flipping a coin
   b. the outcome of a horse race
   c. balancing a checkbook
   d. slot machine

3. The **INT** command means:

   a. integral
   b. intuition
   c. intensity
   d. integer

4. How many pairs of parentheses does the random number formula contain?

    a. zero
    b. one
    c. two
    d. three

5. What numbers will the following yield?

    ```
    LET R = INT(RND(1)*1000+1)
    ```

    a. any whole number between 0 and 999
    b. any whole number between 1 to 1000
    c. any number between 0.6829 and infinity

6. After a random number has been chosen, to get it displayed on the screen you have to tell the computer to:

    a. **RUN**
    b. **WALK**
    c. **PRINT**
    d. **LIST**

9 READ/DATA

Another way to stuff those boxes

Programmers are a notoriously lazy lot. They are constantly seeking new ways to have the computer work for them faster and more efficiently. Since the manipulation of variables and the values within them is some of the most important work a computer does, it stands to reason that programmers would want BASIC to offer several variable-related commands.

In this chapter we'll be learning a new command called **READ/DATA**. It is another paired BASIC command, joining the ranks of **IF/THEN** and **FOR/NEXT**. In function, though, the **READ/DATA** command is more similar to **LET** and **INPUT** because it allows information to be placed into variables.

We are about to learn how to use **READ/DATA** to put a series of values into a variable in a very efficient way. But first let's review how we use **LET** and **INPUT** to place values into variables.

Let's say, for example, we want to put the value "mumbletypeg" into the variable GAME$. Here's how we would do it using the **LET** statement.

179

```
NEW

10 LET GAME$ = "mumbletypeg"
20 PRINT "How about a game of ";GAME$;"?"
```

When we **RUN** this program, we get

```
RUN

How about a game of mumbletypeg?
```

That certainly is an easy way to get a value into a variable. But, as we learned when we were introduced to **LET** in Chapter 4, we are forced to completely rewrite Line 10 if we want to change the value in **GAME$**.

By changing the program slightly, we can set it up so that the user will be asked a question and will himself have the opportunity of putting the value in the variable. That way, the value can be changed without the necessity of rewriting any of the program lines.

We'll do this by using the **INPUT** command (see Chapter 5) as well as an **IF/THEN** statement on Line 30 to weed out incorrect responses. Here's what our new statements would look like.

```
NEW

10 PRINT "What game involves tossing a
   jackknife to the ground";
20 INPUT GAME$
30 IF GAME$ <> "mumbletypeg" THEN PRINT "Sorry,
   it's not ";GAME$;". Try again.": GOTO 10
40 PRINT "Mumbletypeg is absolutely right."
```

When we **RUN** this more complex program, we get

```
RUN

What game involves tossing a jackknife to the
ground? jacks
Sorry, it's not jacks. Try again.
What game involves tossing a jackknife to the
ground? horseshoes
Sorry, it's not horseshoes. Try again.
What game involves tossing a jackknife to the
ground? mumbletypeg
Mumbletypeg is absolutely right.
```

Admittedly, we had to go to more trouble programming it, but this program still manages to get "mumbletypeg" in **GAMES**.

DOING IT WITH READ/DATA

One nice thing about BASIC is the fact that, as a language, it offers the programmer more than one way to accomplish a task. Along with **LET** and **INPUT**, the **READ/DATA** statement provides yet another way to get a value into a variable. It allows the programmer to store a lot of information in a program and control exactly when and where that information is put into the variables.

The **READ/DATA** commands are more compact than **LET**, so you don't have to write an instruction such as

```
LET ANSWER$ = "Shakespeare"
```

every time you want to put a value in a variable. Likewise, **READ/DATA** differs from **INPUT**. With **READ/DATA** the placement of values into variables is automatic rather than interactive and thus is not dependent upon the user.

By way of an introduction to the uses and functions of this new command,

here's how our Mumbletypeg program would look if it were written with
READ/DATA.

```
NEW

10 FOR PASTIME = 1 TO 3
20 READ GAME$
30 PRINT GAME$;" is one swell game."
40 NEXT PASTIME
50 DATA Tetherball,Cribbage,Mumbletypeg
```

That's what it looks like inside the computer. Now let's **RUN** it and see
what it does.

```
RUN

Tetherball is one swell game.
Cribbage is one swell game.
Mumbletypeg is one swell game.
```

And that's it! At first glance it might seem like a lot of work for a relatively
small payoff. Just from looking at the screen, it would be impossible to
distinguish this program from one written with three simple **PRINT** statements instead of this fancy **READ/DATA** command.

But before you pass final judgment, let's take a closer look. You see, this
READ/DATA command is a highly functional one and we're about to examine how it works. Let's take a look at what the computer did when we ran this
program.

So How Did It Do That

In this version of the program, we wanted to have the names of three
games placed into **GAME$**. To make sure that happened, we set up a

FOR/NEXT loop on Line 10.

```
10 FOR PASTIME = 1 TO 3
```

The first command within the confines of the **FOR/NEXT** loop appears on Line 20.

```
20 READ GAME$
```

This is part of our new **READ/DATA** command. When the computer sees Line 20, it receives the following message: "Create a string variable called **GAME$** and put into it the first piece of available data from the first **DATA** line you find."

Since the **READ** line includes a "search and find" aspect to it (the computer must locate the **DATA** line and then fill the variable with data from the line) and since we have three pieces of data to be **READ** into **GAME$**, we want the computer to execute Line 20 three times. This is why Line 20 is inside the **FOR/NEXT** loop.

The next line of our program is Line 30.

```
30 PRINT GAME$;" is one swell game."
```

The computer will take the current value of GAME$ (which, as we will soon see, will be changing) and PRINT it on the screen along with the string " is one swell game." We'll want Line 30 to be PRINTed once for each new word in GAME$. Therefore, we want to make sure that this line, too, is within the jurisdiction of the FOR/NEXT loop.

Okay. That's it for what goes inside of the loop. Now we have to tidy things; we'll end our FOR/NEXT loop on Line 40.

```
40 NEXT PASTIME
```

This line tells the computer to return to the program line that begins with FOR PASTIME (Line 10) and continue the loop.

The last line of the program is the long awaited DATA line.

```
50 DATA Tetherball,Cribbage,Mumbletypeg
```

All the values from Line 50 will be READ into GAME$. Line 50 doesn't need to be inside of the FOR/NEXT loop because it's not really a command to *do* anything; it is just a place where the information is stored. As you can see, this line contains three pieces of data (the names of three games), and each is separated by a comma.

Line 50 is also the place where the computer searches for data while executing Line 20. Since Line 20 activates the data search, it needs to be inside the FOR/NEXT loop, but Line 50 does not.

The Rules of the READ/DATA Game

Now that we've seen the operation of a program that uses READ/DATA, try to remember the following rules about the data found on a DATA line:

· Data may appear *anywhere* in a program but, to conform to proper programming etiquette, is usually placed at the end of a program.

· Data on a single data line may be strings, numbers, or a combination of both.

· The type of variable used on a READ line must match the DATA being read into it (in other words, you can't READ a string into a numeric variable).

· Pieces of data must be separated from each other by commas.

· There are no restrictions on the number of data pieces a DATA line may contain except those restrictions that a particular BASIC uses to determine the length of any statement.

· If data are strings, some BASICs require quotation marks around them.

· If data are numbers, quotation marks are never needed.

What READ Does with DATA

Since **READ/DATA** statements are treated by the computer in a special way, part of understanding them requires learning about this treatment.

As usual, the computer travels from line to line in sequence. However, on reaching the **DATA** line the computer does not execute the line at all. In fact, it completely ignores the line.

The computer notices the **DATA** line only when told to do so by a **READ** line. The **READ** line tells the computer, "Look for a data line."

Here's our program one more time.

```
LIST

10 FOR PASTIME = 1 TO 3
20 READ GAME$
30 PRINT GAME$; " is one swell game."
40 NEXT PASTIME
50 DATA Tetherball,Cribbage,Mumbletypeg
```

It should look more familiar and comfortable to you now.

There's only one other thing you should know. The second time through the loop, the computer knows where it found its last piece of data because it left an "arrow" of sorts there as a pointer. This arrow points to the last read piece of data and prevents the computer from taking a piece of data that has already been taken.

With that pointer in place, the computer continues searching for **DATA** and jumps to Line 50, where it will find "Cribbage" as the next available piece of data to be **READ** into **GAMES**. And this explains why the computer will **PRINT**

```
Cribbage is one swell game.
```

when it has finished **PRINT**ing the "Tetherball" string.

The third time through the loop, the computer will find "Mumbletypeg" as the next available piece of data. The result is that

```
Mumbletypeg is one swell game.
```

appears on the screen. The **FOR/NEXT** loop is completed now and so is the program. When using **READ/DATA**, the filling of variables is automatic. We could have typed in each phrase (as we would have done with **LET** or **INPUT**), but this is much easier.

Out of DATA

If you create a program that **READ**s **DATA** into a variable, you have to make sure that you tell the computer to stop reading when all the data are used up. This can be accomplished with a **FOR/NEXT** loop (which we have just demonstrated), an **IF/THEN** statement (which checks to see if the piece of data just **READ** is the last **DATA** item in the program), or a **RESTORE** command (which we will demonstrate in the last program of this chapter).

If you don't stop the computer from trying to **READ** nonexisting **DATA**, you could end up with an **OUT OF DATA ERROR**, as in the following program:

```
NEW

10 FOR ODE = 1 TO 4
20 READ POEM$
30 PRINT POEM$
40 NEXT ODE
50 DATA The Wasteland,Song of Myself,The Fog
```

Here's what happens when we **RUN** this program.

```
RUN

The Wasteland
Song of Myself
The Fog

OUT OF DATA ERROR IN 20
```

The program is stopped with an error because it was trying to **READ** four pieces of **DATA** (as instructed in Line 10) and there were only three pieces in the program.

READ/DATA WITH NUMBERS

The **READ/DATA** command lends itself very nicely to numbers. If, for example, you want to write a program that shows how different given values affect the outcome of a formula, **READ/DATA** would be the ideal command to use. Let's try one.

Since gasoline and soft drinks are now being sold by the liter, we'll keep in step with the movement to be more scientific in measuring quantities and create a program that converts Fahrenheit temperatures into Celsius.

Our handy Webster's dictionary tells us that a Fahrenheit temperature may be converted to its Celsius equivalent by using this formula (where F equals the degrees of the Fahrenheit temperature and C equals the degrees on the Celsius scale):

F = 9/5C + 32

This formula tells us we can figure out the Fahrenheit temperature by taking the Celsius temperature, multiplying it by nine-fifths, and adding 32 to the results.

Hmmm. So that's how it's done. All right, we can feed that into a computer (in the form of a **LET** statement). To make the program work, we will also have to create some Fahrenheit values and store them on a DATA line.

To organize the display, we could have the computer PRINT some Fahrenheit temperatures on the left side of the screen and their corresponding Celsius temperatures on the right. Sounds like a worthwhile endeavor. Let's write a program that does just that.

Will You Need Earmuffs When It's 16 C?

To begin our program, let's create two column headings under which all of our temperatures will be PRINTed. We'll have a left hand column called FAHRENHEIT and a right hand column called CELSIUS. The computer will happily display these two words for us when it receives an instruction like this one.

```
10 PRINT "FAHRENHEIT    CELSIUS"
```

Notice that there are four spaces between the "T" and the "C." These spaces are needed because (as we will explain on Line 50) we will be creating two columns of temperatures by separating them with a comma in a PRINT statement.

In a BASIC that separates its PRINT columns by 14 spaces, all the Fahrenheit temperatures will be PRINTed in a column that begins under the "F" and all the Celsius temperatures will be PRINTed in a column that begins under the "C."

Once again, there's going to be a FOR/NEXT loop in this program. Please note that the PRINT statement on Line 10 is *not* going to be within that loop because we only want the FAHRENHEIT and CELSIUS column headings to be PRINTed *once*.

We frequently need a FOR/NEXT loop with a READ/DATA statement to keep count of the number of data pieces. Therefore, the next thing we should decide, in putting this program together, is how many pieces of data we want to include on our DATA line. Ten is a nice round number. Let's go with that. Now we can set up our FOR/NEXT loop for the numbers 1 to 10.

```
20 FOR TEMP = 1 TO 10
```

That's fine. We have the beginning of a **FOR/NEXT** loop that is going to put the numbers 1 through 10 into a numeric variable called **TEMP**. (We had planned to call the variable **TEMPERATURE**. But since **AT** is a reserved word in some BASICs, we had to settle for **TEMP**.)

Now let's enter a **READ** line.

```
30 READ FAHRENHEIT
```

Line 30 tells the computer that a numeric variable called **FAHRENHEIT** will be used to store pieces of data (Fahrenheit temperatures) from a **DATA** line. Line 30 needs to be placed inside the boundaries of the **FOR/NEXT** loop because we are telling the computer to **READ** ten values into **FAHRENHEIT**. That means the computer has to visit the **READ** line (Line 30) ten different times in order to grab ten pieces of data.

The next line is going to take that conversion formula from the dictionary (reversed so that we'll be able to plug in our known Fahrenheit values to figure out the unknown Celsius values) and convert it into BASIC. Line 40 looks like this.

```
40 LET CELSIUS = 5/9 * (FAHRENHEIT - 32)
```

Line 40 tells the computer to subtract 32 from the Fahrenheit value and then multiply the result by five-ninths (5 divided by 9).

Now, with the heavy work out of the way (and the computer programmed to do all of it), we need to create a line that's going to **PRINT** the results for us, one that will translate those Fahrenheit values into Celsius. Let's enter

```
50 PRINT FAHRENHEIT, CELSIUS
```

This line tells the computer to **PRINT** the values of **FAHRENHEIT** and **CELSIUS** each time it reaches Line 50. (Because Line 50 is within the **FOR/NEXT** loop, the computer will be showing up ten times to **PRINT** those values.)

Notice that we've used a comma to separate the two variables. If you recall from Chapter 3, a comma in a **PRINT** statement not enclosed in quotation marks has the effect of spacing things out. In Line 50, the precise effect is this: It tells our computer to **PRINT** the two values of **FAHRENHEIT** and **CELSIUS** 14 horizontal spaces apart on the same line. (As we mentioned before, the number of spaces separating the columns will differ from computer to computer.)

Line 60 is the end of our **FOR/NEXT** loop, and it looks like this.

```
60 NEXT TEMP
```

Line 60 tells the computer to return to the program line that begins with **FOR TEMP** (Line 20) and put the next number in the sequence into **TEMP**.

Finally, we now need to put in all the data (Fahrenheit values) that we want the computer to plug into our handy formula on Line 40.

So let's create two **DATA** lines with some typical Fahrenheit temperatures whose Celsius equivalents we've always wanted to reveal.

```
70 DATA 93,-20,32,212,1
80 DATA 81,14,50,40,-10
```

Notice that this time we put the data on two separate **DATA** lines. We didn't have to do it this way, but we wanted to show you that data can be separated on different lines.

The computer will **READ** in all the data beginning on Line 70. When it comes to the last piece of data on the line, the computer will search for the next piece of data in the program and automatically drop down to Line 80 to **READ** more data.

In this case, the computer doesn't have far to search. We gave our two **DATA** lines consecutive line numbers in this program, but they don't need to be consecutive.

Lines 70 and 80 do not need to be within the **FOR/NEXT** loop. A **DATA** line can literally be *anywhere* in the program but, in keeping with convention, we placed it at the very end. The **DATA** line can be outside of the loop because it serves as a pickup station for data.

Even though the computer will need to go to Line 70 and then to Line 80 (to pick up all ten pieces of data), the **READ** command (Line 30) sends it there. Therefore, **READ** is the one that needs to be within the loop, not **DATA**.

Now that we understand the game plan, we are prepared to **LIST** our complete program and take a good look at it.

```
LIST

10 PRINT "FAHRENHEIT    CELSIUS"
20 FOR TEMP = 1 TO 10
30 READ FAHRENHEIT
40 LET CELSIUS = 5/9 * (FAHRENHEIT - 32)
50 PRINT FAHRENHEIT, CELSIUS
60 NEXT TEMP
70 DATA 93,-20,32,212,1
80 DATA 81,14,50,40,-10
```

Good. Now let's RUN it (and be prepared for all kinds of weather).

```
RUN

FAHRENHEIT    CELSIUS
93            33.88888888
-20           -28.88888888
32            0
212           99.999999999
1             -17.222222222
81            27.222222221
14            -9.99999999
50            9.99999999
40            4.44444444
-10           -23.33333333
```

It looks impressive, but we could do without those decimals. Let's use the same INT command that helped us out in Chapter 8 and turn all these temperatures into *whole numbers*. (We do this because, for our purposes here, we don't need to be laboratory exact with our figures; besides, who can honestly relate to 0.22222221 of a degree?)

Here's the instruction that will give us whole numbers.

```
45 LET CELSIUS = INT(CELSIUS + 0.5)
```

This line tells the computer to "round off" the value of CELSIUS (which it figured out on Line 40). The computer does this by first adding 0.5 to the value and then calculating the next lower whole number value. This new number becomes the current value of CELSIUS.

If the number has a decimal greater than or equal to 0.5, the computer rounds the number *up*, raising the temperature to the next whole number. Otherwise, it rounds the number *down* by dropping off the decimal. Now our program will be able to take those Celsius values and make them into whole numbers.

Let's LIST the program again with the inclusion of Line 45.

```
LIST

10 PRINT "FAHRENHEIT    CELSIUS"
20 FOR TEMPERATURE = 1 TO 10
30 READ FAHRENHEIT
40 LET CELSIUS = 5/9 * (FAHRENHEIT - 32)
45 LET CELSIUS = INT(CELSIUS + 0.5)
50 PRINT FAHRENHEIT, CELSIUS
60 NEXT TEMP
70 DATA 93,-20,32,212,1
80 DATA 81,14,50,40,-10
```

Now when we **RUN** it, the values will be easier for us nonscientific types to appreciate.

```
RUN

FAHRENHEIT      CELSIUS
93              34
-20             -29
32              0
212             100
1               -17
81              27
14              -10
50              10
40              4
-10             -23
```

There. That's better. One more thing before we sign off here. You should know, in case you haven't already assumed as much, that to alter the Fahrenheit values all you have to do is change the values on the **DATA** line.

We could, for example, rewrite Lines 70 and 80 to get

```
70 DATA 17,106,-250,39,75
80 DATA 69,350,0,99,61
```

then **LIST** the program to get

```
LIST

10 PRINT "FAHRENHEIT    CELSIUS"
20 FOR TEMP = 1 TO 10
30 READ FAHRENHEIT
40 LET CELSIUS = 5/9 * (FAHRENHEIT - 32)
45 LET CELSIUS = INT(CELSIUS + 0.5)
50 PRINT FAHRENHEIT, CELSIUS
60 NEXT TEMP
70 DATA 17,106,-250,39,75
80 DATA 69,350,0,99,61
```

and **RUN** it to get

```
RUN

FAHRENHEIT    CELSIUS
17            -8
106           41
-250          -157
39            4
75            24
69            21
350           177
0             -18
99            37
61            16
```

As you can see from the last Fahrenheit and Celsius values displayed in the preceding columns, you will *not* need your earmuffs when it's 16 degrees Celsius.

So there you have it. The hot and the cold of it. The **READ** and the **DATA** of it. Now, before we close this chapter, we want to show you one more program—one that illustrates a slightly more sophisticated use of **READ/DATA**.

WHO'S CALLING, PLEASE

We have included this final **READ/DATA** program to show you a more practical application. We'll show how the computer can be instructed to search through a program for a specific piece of data. Hold on, here comes the complete listing.

```
10 PRINT:PRINT "Whose phone number do you want";
20 INPUT WHO$
30 RESTORE
40 FOR SEARCH = 1 TO 4
50 READ NAME$,TELPHN$,AGE
60 IF WHO$ = NAME$ THEN GOTO 90
70 NEXT SEARCH
80 PRINT "I don't have ";WHO$;"'s name on file,
   try again.":GOTO 10
90 PRINT WHO$;"'s phone is ";TELPHN$
100 PRINT WHO$;"'s age is ";AGE
110 END
500 DATA Vincent,888-1853,37
510 DATA Rembrandt,777-1606,63
520 DATA Chagall,333-1889,93
530 DATA Pablo,666-1881,92
```

Before we attempt to explain the inner workings of this masterpiece of telephone technology par excellence, we're going to **RUN** it for you and give you an opportunity to watch it in action.

```
RUN

Whose phone number do you want? Jessica
I don't have Jessica's name on file, try again.

Whose phone number do you want? Chagall
Chagall's phone is 333-1889
Chagall's age is 93
```

And let's try it once again.

```
RUN


Whose phone number do you want? Scot
I don't have Scot's name on file, try again.

Whose phone number do you want? Vincent
Vincent's phone is 888-1853
Vincent's age is 37
```

This program employs **READ/DATA** as a "search and find" command and gives the computer the role of a telephone operator. When the user types in a name, the computer searches through the four names in the telephone "file" looking for the desired one.

If it finds the name, the person's phone number and age are **PRINT**ed. If it doesn't, the computer tells the user the desired name can't be found and lets the user try another name.

Now that you've seen the program working a few times, let's dissect it and find out how it's doing what it's doing.

To begin with, we have

```
10 PRINT:PRINT "Whose phone number do you want";
```

Line 10 contains two **PRINT** statements separated by a colon. The first **PRINT** will enable the computer to **PRINT** a blank line. The second **PRINT** will display the text of the question, "Whose phone number do you want?"

Continuing to the next line, we have

```
20 INPUT WHO$
```

In Line 20 the **INPUT** command is followed by **WHO$**, the string variable that will accept the answer to the question.

When the screen displays

```
30 RESTORE
```

we meet a command we have not seen before. Used only in conjunction with **READ/DATA**, **RESTORE** means the imaginary arrow that always indicates the next available piece of data will now be reset so that it is poised at the beginning of the program.

In other words, when the computer sees the **RESTORE** command, it is told, "Now you can access all of the program's data all over again." The **RESTORE** command is unnecessary in a program unless you plan to "recycle" the data and use it all again (as we will be doing in this program).

The next line in the program is

```
40 FOR SEARCH = 1 TO 4
```

Line 40 establishes a **FOR/NEXT** loop, determining that four trips will be taken in search of data.

When we arrive at

```
50 READ NAME$,TELPHN$,AGE
```

we find a **READ** line containing the variables **NAME$**, **TELPHN$**, and **AGE**, each needing to be filled with information. A **READ** line like this one deals with three variables at one time.

When the computer looks for **DATA** for these variables, it will be picking up three pieces of data (called *data triplets*) with each visit to the **DATA** line. The first piece it finds will go in the first variable (**NAME$**). The second piece from the **DATA** line will go into the second variable (**TELPHN$**). And the third piece of data will go into the third variable (**AGE**).

Once the computer reaches

```
60 IF WHO$ = NAME$ THEN GOTO 90
```

it learns what to do **IF** the name of the person whose phone number is being requested *is* equal to the value in **NAME$**. In other words, **IF** the names match, **THEN** the computer will **GOTO** Line 90.

```
90 PRINT WHO$;"'s phone is ";TELPHN$
100 PRINT WHO$;"'s age is ";AGE
110 END
```

Line 90 will **PRINT** the person's phone number and take the computer down to Line 100, which will **PRINT** the person's age. At Line 110 the program will end. Actually, the program would end here even if we didn't use Line 110, since **DATA** lines aren't actually executed. Its presense is just to add a little more clarity to the program.

As you probably noticed, we skipped over a few lines there. Let's return to Line 60 and pick them up in our explanation.

Now, **IF** the condition on Line 60 is false (in other words, if the name that was requested is *not* the current name in **NAME$**), **THEN** the computer will proceed to

```
70 NEXT SEARCH
```

Line 70, with its **NEXT SEARCH** command, tells the computer to go back to the **FOR SEARCH** line (Line 40) and then to Line 50 where it will fill the three variables with the next three data triplets.

This **READ**ing in process will continue until **WHO$** equals **NAMES$** or the computer has exhausted all the data triplets. When the latter happens, the computer will exit the **FOR/NEXT** loop and execute

```
80 PRINT "I don't have ";WHO$;"'s name on file,
   try again.":GOTO 10
```

Line 80 informs the user that the person he or she is trying to contact has an unlisted number. The final command on Line 80 tells the computer to **GOTO** 10, where the original question, "Whose phone number do you want?", will be asked again.

After the question is asked, the computer will (on Line 30) **RESTORE** all the data, and the search process will begin all over again.

That's how the program works. As you can see, it really wasn't quite as bad as it looked, and it certainly showed off the impressive capabilities of the versatile **READ/DATA** command.

SUMMARY

The paired command **READ/DATA** is the third of three ways that we've explored in this book to put information into a variable. Although **LET** will allow a programmer to put a value into a variable, using a **LET** statement can be a hassle if the value needs to be changed.

On the other hand, **INPUT** makes for easy changing of values. But since it is interactive, the programmer has no control over the values the user **INPUT**s.

That leaves **READ/DATA**. A beautiful command, it not only allows the programmer to specify the values to be put in a variable, but also puts them in with the greatest of ease. And if that isn't enough to make **READ/DATA** one of a programmer's most useful tools, this command also makes the changing of dozens of pieces of data as simple as rewriting a single **DATA** line.

9 QUIZ

1. The **READ/DATA** allows a programmer to put a value into:
    a. an **INPUT** statement
    b. a bargain
    c. a variable

2. In order to keep count of the data on a **DATA** line, the **READ/DATA** command is often accompanied by a:
    a. **GOTO** loop
    b. **FOR/NEXT** loop
    c. loop-the-loop

3. There is a syntax error on which one of the following lines:

```
10 FOR IDEA = 1 TO 3
20 READ ANSWER$
30 PRINT ANSWER$
40 NIX IDEA
50 DATA "biofocals";"adhesive";"falsh eyelashes"
```

4. Data on a **DATA** line can be a mixture of numbers and strings: True or False?

5. The computer will only look at a **DATA** line after it has been commanded to by:

   a. **READ**
   b. **GOTO**
   c. court order

6. When listing strings on a **DATA** line, the strings must be:

   a. tied
   b. enclosed in quotation marks
   c. separated by commas

7. A **DATA** line may appear at which location in a program:

   a. the beginning
   b. the middle
   c. the end
   d. all of the above

10 **GOSUB**

Subroutines: Programming efficiently

There comes a time in the course of computer-generated events when the simplest and most efficiently constructed solution is the best. Good programmers always strive to make their programs clear and readable. (Perhaps a desire for immortality leads us all to believe that centuries from now our programs will survive.)

That being the case, we should aim to produce a well-written program, and when that has been accomplished, we'll have something to make us proud.

We have explored many BASIC commands and concepts in this book, but the *subroutine* is probably the greatest aid in creating coherent programs.

With subroutines you can write a program the logic of which even a beginner can follow. Without them, long programs tend to be jumbled and difficult for any human to decipher.

203

WHAT A SUBROUTINE IS

A subroutine is a line or lines of instruction that can be used to perform a specified task many times within a program. BASIC allows us to put these lines under an "umbrella" called a subroutine.

Whenever we need to have that specified task performed, all we have to do is tell the computer to **GOSUB**. This command literally means, "Go to the subroutine," and it is followed by the line number on which the subroutine begins. If, for example, we have a subroutine that begins on Line 500, we can send the computer there with

```
10 GOSUB 500
```

When the computer finishes the work of the subroutine, it will be ready to execute your next command.

Why They Are So Useful

Since they can easily be linked together, subroutines are often thought of as a program's *building blocks*. When creating a large program, the programmer is likely to devote certain sections or blocks of instructional code to certain tasks within the program. By working with several of these blocks, or subprograms, a large programming job is much easier to tackle.

Subroutines are also valuable in another way. They make it easier for a programmer to find errors. You see, even the best programmers expect some trouble while they are writing their programs.

The "trouble" usually takes the form of some undesired result that inexplicably shows up during the creation and testing process. These results are unceremoniously called bugs, and "debugging" is an activity with which every programmer is all too familiar.

Since subroutines can be thought of as independent subprograms, bugs occurring within any of them can (hopefully) be easily isolated and remedied. In other words, it's easier to pinpoint a bug that is hiding in a small subroutine than one hiding in the endless nooks and crannies of a large program.

Programming Without GOSUB

Some programs require the repetition of a single task. Depending on its extensiveness and degree of repetition, a single task could mean a lot of work for the programmer. Here's an example of one that certainly repeats itself.

```
NEW

10 PRINT "Old MacDonald had a farm,"
20 PRINT "EEAI, EEAI OH!"
30 PRINT "And on his farm he had some ducks,"
40 PRINT "EEAI, EEAI OH!"
50 PRINT "With a quack quack here and a quack
   quack there."
60 PRINT "Here a quack, there a quack, everywhere
   a quack quack."
70 PRINT "Old MacDonald had a farm,"
80 PRINT "EEAI, EEAI OH!"
```

Now that's a program crying out for a subroutine if ever we've seen one. We'll fix it up in a minute, but let's **RUN** it before we do (please feel free to sing along).

```
RUN

Old MacDonald had a farm,
EEAI, EEAI OH!
And on his farm he had some ducks,
EEAI, EEAI OH!
With a quack quack here and a quack quack there.
Here a quack, there a quack, everywhere a quack quack.
Old MacDonald had a farm,
EEAI, EEAI OH!
```

Programming "Old MacDonald" was definitely too much work! Now let's see what it would take to write the same program with a subroutine.

GOSUB—THERE AND BACK AGAIN

To put your mind at ease, there is nothing unusual about the commands placed in a subroutine. (As you will see shortly, all are familiar commands.)

To place a subroutine in a program all you have to do is isolate a task within the program (perhaps something that is going to be used over and over, like "EEAI, EEAI OH!"), and write the instructions for it.

Whenever you want the computer to execute (or "call up") the subroutine, you simply use the **GOSUB** command. Here's the improved version of our little program.

```
NEW

10 PRINT "Old MacDonald had a farm,"
20 GOSUB 100
30 PRINT "And on his farm he had some ducks,"
40 GOSUB 100
50 PRINT "With a quack quack here and a quack
   quack there."
60 PRINT "Here a quack, there a quack, everywhere
   a quack quack."
70 PRINT "Old MacDonald had a farm,"
80 GOSUB 100
90 END
100 PRINT "EEAI, EEAI OH!"
110 RETURN
```

Now let's follow the line of logic that the computer must take to execute this program. Each time the computer reaches a line that says **GOSUB** 100, it will jump to Line 100 and **PRINT** "EEAI, EEAI OH!"

After it is done with Line 100, the computer will go to Line 110, which says **RETURN** and thus signals the end of the subroutine.

When the computer **RETURN**s, it will always **RETURN** to the command *following* the **GOSUB** that sent it to the subroutine. For example, in the program above, the computer will first be sent to Line 100 by the **GOSUB** 100 command on Line 20.

When the computer **RETURN**s from the subroutine, it will **RETURN** to the command *after* Line 20, and that puts it on Line 30. From Line 30, it will go to Line 40 and, from there, it will jump to Line 100 again. This time, when it **RETURN**s, it will **RETURN** to the command *after* Line 40, and that means Line 50.

Lines 50, 60, and 70 will be **PRINT**ed in succession. When the computer reaches Line 80, it will be sent to the subroutine for the last time. Upon **RETURN**ing this time, it will go to Line 90, which simply tells the computer to **END**. And that is the **END** of the song (at least as far as we go).

Now that we've explained it, there should be no surprises about the outcome when we **RUN** the following program. (For those who do not consider this one of your old favorites, please bear with us.)

```
RUN

Old MacDonald had a farm,
EEAI, EEAI OH!
And on his farm he had some ducks,
EEAI, EEAI OH!
With a quack quack here and a quack quack there.
Here a quack, there a quack, everywhere a quack quack.
Old MacDonald had a farm,
EEAI, EEAI OH!
```

Now that you're warmed up, we hate to stop here. But we think you get the idea. As you can see, this **RUN** is identical to the preceding one. However, there is a major difference. The first program lacks the conciseness that the second program achieves by using a subroutine.

Subroutines and the Law

As with the use of all BASIC commands and concepts, syntax (etiquette, if you will) must be observed. Before we move on to some more sophisticated uses of subroutines, we would do well to examine some of the fundamental rules regarding them (to avoid public embarrassment over using a semicolon instead of a colon).

Although you'll probably never see these rules referred to in this manner anywhere else, we call them the Seven Laws of Subroutines. When working with subroutines, try to observe the following:

1. A program may have any number of subroutines.

2. A subroutine can consist of any number of lines containing any bona fide BASIC commands.

3. Subroutines can be placed *anywhere* in a program, but convention usually groups them at the very end, right *before* the **DATA** lines if there are any.

4. A subroutine should only be executed by a **GOSUB** command, which literally means, "Go to the subroutine" (just as a **DATA** line can only be accessed by a **READ** command).

5. The end of a subroutine is always marked with a **RETURN** command. This command means, "Return to the command right *after* the **GOSUB** command, and carry on from there."

6. The main body of the program is most frequently separated from a subroutine by an **END** statement. This statement means, "This is the end of the regular program; when you get to this line, *stop*."

7. Subroutines can be called from within other subroutines.

If you study these rules and refer back to Old MacDonald, you should have no problem with what lies ahead.

EXPANDING THE PLOT—A LITERATURE QUIZ

We are now about to undertake another program that makes use of a subroutine. Here's the plan. We're going to create a little literature quiz. The user will be asked three questions and will then have to select the correct answer from among three choices (sounds like our end of chapter quizzes).

Each time the question is answered correctly, the computer will offer congratulations, give the user one point, and present the next question. When the answer is incorrect, the computer will say so, provide the correct answer, and go on to the next question.

This program will have three variables (all numeric). They will be used to store three different kinds of information relating to the program.

One variable (**POINTS**) will store the number of points the user has accumulated for correct answers. Another (**ANSWER**) will store the user's answers. And the third (**RIGHTANSR**) will store the preprogrammed correct answer to each question. Now that you have some idea about what we're trying to do, let's begin.

As we mentioned in the preceding statement, we are going to be keeping score in this test; therefore, we need to create a variable that is going to store the points the user accumulates.

This may sound difficult, but it's really just a matter of using a **LET** statement. Placed on Line 10, the statement says

```
NEW

10 LET POINTS = 0
```

We have arbitrarily chosen the name **POINTS** for our numeric variable. We have given it a value of 0 because at the beginning of this test, or any test, the student's grade is 0.

After the first question that is answered correctly, the computer will be adding 1 to this original 0 value and then another 1 after the second correct question, and so forth. The maximum score for our quiz is three points.

Okay, now let's write our first question for the quiz. Since this is a test of literary knowledge, we'll start with a question whose answer the user may know. In this way we can reduce any test anxiety that might be present. Line 20 looks like this.

```
20 PRINT "Pinocchio's father was 1) Giradoux 2) Geppetto
   3) Giant Sequoia";
```

Usually when we **PRINT** a question, we immediately want to give the user an opportunity to answer it. But this time we're going to hold off with the **INPUT** statement for a moment and, instead, create one other line to follow Line 20.

It's going to be a **LET** statement that tells the computer to create a numeric variable called **RIGHTANSR** (standing for **RIGHT ANSweR**) and to place in it the value 2 (which is the correct answer to the first question). Here's Line 30.

```
30 LET RIGHTANSR = 2
```

With a value established for **RIGHTANSR**, the computer will later be able to compare the user's **INPUT** to the correct answer.

Now that the computer "knows" the correct answer, we're ready to give the user a chance to answer the question. For this, we need an **INPUT** statement followed by a numeric variable. Let's use **ANSWER** for the varia-ble. Here's where the beauty of the subroutine comes to light. Since we're going to have three questions in this program, the line with the instruction **INPUT ANSWER** is going to have to be written three different times *unless* we put the **INPUT ANSWER** command inside a subroutine and send the comput-er to it every time we need it.

Sounds like a great idea! Let's arbitrarily choose Line 500 for the begin-ning of the subroutine. We've picked a number that seems as if it's going to be way at the end of the program, so we should have plenty of line numbers to use before we get there. To get the computer to Line 500, we need the following command:

```
40 GOSUB 500
```

Since we have the computer going to Line 500, let's follow its path of logic and next create the instruction that it will find on arriving at Line 500.

```
500 INPUT ANSWER
```

Although Line 500 is the first instruction of our subroutine, it should not look alien to you. It is a simple **INPUT** statement followed by the numeric variable **ANSWER** and will be used *to accept the answers to each of our three questions.*

In order to let the user know whether he or she has chosen the correct answer, we need to have the computer analyze the contents of **ANSWER** and compare them to the contents of **RIGHTANSR** (which we established on Line 30). This can be done on Line 510 with the following **IF/THEN** statement:

```
510 IF ANSWER <> RIGHTANSR THEN PRINT "Sorry, the
    answer is ";RIGHTANSR : GOTO 530
```

As you can see, this conditional statement tells the computer what to do **IF** the user's answer is *not* equal to the correct answer. It tells the computer "**IF** the answer is incorrect, **THEN PRINT** your regrets, reveal the correct answer, *and* **GOTO** Line 530." (We'll be showing you Line 530 in a minute; let's just take a look at Line 520 first.)

Line 520 is going to tell the computer what to do if the user's answer *is* correct. Here's what it looks like.

```
520 PRINT "GREAT!": LET POINTS = POINTS + 1
```

Line 520 will be executed *only* **IF** the user's answer is the correct one. (As we explained on Line 510, **IF** the answer is incorrect, the computer will detour around Line 520 and go to Line 530.)

That being the case, the computer will **PRINT** "Great!" for every correct answer *and* will increment (increase) the variable **POINTS** (which we first used on Line 10) by 1. Every time the condition on Line 520 is true (that is, the answer is correct), the computer will add one point to the user's grade.

Although **LET POINTS = POINTS + 1** looks like an equation (in the algebraic sense), it is *not an equality*. (A value plus 1 could never be equal to the original value.) Line 520 tells the computer, "Create a numeric variable called **POINTS** and set it equal to the former value of **POINTS** plus one additional point."

This **LET POINTS = POINTS + 1** statement is called an *incrementer,* or more simply a *counter,* and is commonly used in BASIC programs.

We have finished all of the important work of the subroutine, and now we just have to complete a few details. Line 530 (which is where the computer goes when the answer is incorrect) tells the computer to **PRINT** a blank line.

```
530 PRINT
```

This command will **PRINT** a blank line to visually separate each of the questions. Now we've reached the end of our subroutine, so we need a **RETURN** command. Let's put it on Line 540.

```
540 RETURN
```

Let's **LIST** what we have so far.

```
LIST

10 LET POINTS = 0
20 PRINT "Pinocchio's father was 1) Giradoux 2) Geppetto
   3) Giant Sequoia";
30 LET RIGHTANSR = 2
40 GOSUB 500
500 INPUT ANSWER
510 IF ANSWER <> RIGHTANSR THEN PRINT "Sorry, the
    answer is ";RIGHTANSR : GOTO 530
520 PRINT "GREAT!": LET POINTS = POINTS + 1
530 PRINT
540 RETURN
```

Okay, now where were we? Ah, yes. The computer had just reached Line 540 and received the command to **RETURN**. All right, now let's see who's been paying close attention. Where does the computer go after reading **RETURN**? To figure this one out, we have to look back and see on what line the **GOSUB 500** command appears. It is Line 40. So the line that comes after Line 40 is Line 50. Alas, there is no Line 50 at the moment, but we can fix that.

Line 50 is the text of the quiz's second question. It looks like this.

```
50 PRINT "The Old Man and the Sea was written by
   1) Hemingway 2) Melville 3) Beethoven";
```

Following our question on Line 50, we need to tell the computer what the correct answer is (as we did on Line 30). To do this, we recycle **RIGHTANSR** and give it a new value.

```
60 LET RIGHTANSR = 1
```

Now that the computer knows the correct answer for Question Number 2, we have to give the user a crack at it also. It's time to use our subroutine on Line 500 again. Now isn't that great? We don't have to rewrite those statements.

Using programming technology, all we have to do to get the computer to analyze the second answer is send it down to the subroutine again. Line 70 does just that.

```
70 GOSUB 500
```

That certainly was easy. Now since we know that the computer is going to go to Line 500 and then to Lines 510, 520, 530, and 540, the next line we write is going to be Line 80, the one to which the computer **RETURN**s after its second trip through the subroutine. Line 80 contains the text of the third and final question.

```
80 PRINT "Bilbo Baggins was hired as a 1) programmer
   2) soda jerk 3) thief";
```

Once again, our question needs to be followed by a new value for **RIGHTANSR**.

```
90 LET RIGHTANSR = 3
```

From there we send the computer down to the subroutine on Line 500 one last time by entering

```
100 GOSUB 500
```

When the analysis work is all done this time, the computer will **RETURN** to Line 110 where we will tell it to **PRINT** an extra blank line.

```
110 PRINT
```

Since this is the end of the quiz, Line 120 is going to be the place where the computer will pass out the grades. Here's how it will be done.

```
120 PRINT "The quiz is over. Your grade is ";POINTS
```

That's all there is except for one last little thing. Because the line after 120 is 500 (the beginning of our first subroutine), we need something to separate the two parts of the problem. Peeking back at Rule Number 6 of the "Seven Laws of Subroutines," we recall that an **END** statement is an appropriate separator at times like this. Let's put one of them on Line 130 and then we'll have no problems.

```
130 END
```

As you probably recall, **END** tells the computer, "This is the end, and after this there is nothing more to do."

What It Looks Like Now

Perhaps you've noticed that we didn't exactly enter our line numbers in numerical sequence while we were writing our program. That's true and it's not a matter of concern because the computer does not mind in which order the line numbers are entered.

When we **LIST** the program, everything will, of course, be displayed in its proper place. But while it is true that you don't always have to plan every aspect of your program ahead of time, it is a good idea to start any subroutine at a high line number.

If you give your subroutine a line number that is too low and the main body of your program starts encroaching on the subroutine, you might have to reenter part or all of it with different line numbers.

Now we are ready to take a look at this program. With 18 lines it is certainly our most sophisticated piece of programming ingenuity to date.

```
LIST

10 LET POINTS = 0
20 PRINT "Pinocchio's father was 1) Giradoux 2) Geppetto
   3) Giant Sequoia";
30 LET RIGHTANSR = 2
40 GOSUB 500
50 PRINT "The Old Man and the Sea was written by
   1) Hemingway 2) Melville 3) Beethoven";
60 LET RIGHTANSR = 1
70 GOSUB 500
80 PRINT "Bilbo Baggins was hired as a 1) programmer
   2) soda jerk 3) thief";
90 LET RIGHTANSR = 3
100 GOSUB 500
110 PRINT
120 PRINT "The quiz is over. Your grade is ";POINTS
130 END
500 INPUT ANSWER
510 IF ANSWER <> RIGHTANSR THEN PRINT "Sorry, the
    answer is ";RIGHTANSR : GOTO 530
520 PRINT "GREAT!": LET POINTS = POINTS + 1
530 PRINT
540 RETURN
```

Now we can see what all this programming is going to yield. Let's **RUN** it, play the part of the naive user, and see what happens. For a programmer at any level of expertise, there is nothing that gives a greater sense of satisfaction than writing something that works (except for being able to purchase a new piece of hardware from your software royalties).

```
RUN

Pinocchio's father was 1) Giradoux 2) Geppetto
   3) Giant Sequoia? 2
GREAT!

The Old Man and the Sea was written by 1) Hemingway
   2) Melville 3) Beethoven? 2
Sorry, the answer is 1

Bilbo Baggins was hired as a 1) programmer 2) soda jerk
   3) thief? 1
Sorry, the answer is 3

The quiz is over. Your grade is 1.
```

A Few Remarks About REMarks

The program is perfect, except...Well, there is one other thing that would make it better. It's something called a *remark* statement, or **REM** in BASIC. Now we know that this is almost the end of the book and you've just finished assimilating all this new information about subroutines. Even so, we would be remiss in our responsibilities if we didn't tell you about **REM**.

A remark in a program is a note that the programmer makes to himself or herself or any other human who might look at the LISTing. The note usually explains the purpose of a certain section of instructions.

These REMarks are not for computers. In fact, when the computer comes to a line that begins with **REM**, it immediately skips over it (the way you would pass over a letter that was addressed to someone else).

Your **REMarks** simply help document a program. When you look back over your LISTing several months or years from now, the **REMarks** should, theoretically, refresh your memory and understanding of the program.

Here are a few **REMarks** we could add to our program. They should need

no explanation. (Please remember, remarks are not going to have the slightest effect on the way the program RUNs.)

```
5 REM - A Literary Quiz by Annie Fox 1982
7 REM - POINTS stores points for correct answers
25 REM - RIGHTANSR stores correct answers
109 REM - Final score PRINTed
499 REM - Subroutine to accept and analyze user INPUT
```

As you can see, these little REMarks really do a lot to explain the functions of the different parts of the program. Notice that they are written in English without any regard for BASIC syntax. The only thing required is that all REMarks be preceded by the REM command.

Let's LIST the whole program now, and have the computer display these REMarks in their correct places.

```
LIST

5 REM - A Literary Quiz by Annie Fox 1982
7 REM - POINTS stores points for correct answers
10 LET POINTS = 0
20 PRINT "Pinocchio's father was 1) Giradoux 2) Geppetto
   3) Giant Sequoia";
25 REM - RIGHTANSR stores correct answers
30 LET RIGHTANSR = 2
40 GOSUB 500
50 PRINT "The Old Man and the Sea was written by
   1) Hemingway 2) Melville 3) Beethoven";
60 LET RIGHTANSR = 1
70 GOSUB 500
80 PRINT "Bilbo Baggins was hired as a 1) programmer
   2) soda jerk 3) thief";
90 LET RIGHTANSR = 3
100 GOSUB 500
109 REM - Final score PRINTed
110 PRINT
120 PRINT "The quiz is over. Your grade is ";POINTS
130 END
499 REM - Subroutine to accept and analyze user INPUT
500 INPUT ANSWER
510 IF ANSWER <> RIGHTANSR THEN PRINT "Sorry, the
    answer is ";RIGHTANSR : GOTO 530
520 PRINT "GREAT!": LET POINTS = POINTS + 1
530 PRINT
540 RETURN
```

The program is complete, and so is this chapter on subroutines.

SUMMARY

Subroutines are the programmer's way of creating efficient programs that are easy for humans (and computers) to read and understand. They permit the creation of programming modules (each with a distinct function) that are a pleasure to test and debug if need be. Subroutines can be as long or as short as you like, and can be called up (with the GOSUB command) toll-free at any time.

A LITTLE POMP AND CIRCUMSTANCE

Since this is the conclusion of the tutorial section of this book, we would like to say we're proud of all of you who made it to this point. You have learned a lot; the first phase of your BASIC programming education is now complete.

So here is your diploma with our congratulations. What you decide to do with what you've learned is, of course, up to you. You now have a solid foundation and are in a good position to continue your exploration of computers (we've really only scratched the surface of BASIC).

In the next chapter, you'll get a look at the future of computers and what you see there just might give you an idea or two with which to play around. Good luck!

10 QUIZ

1. A subprogram within the body of the main BASIC program is called a:
   a. subscript
   b. subroutine
   c. subsidy

2. The BASIC command used to call up a subroutine is:
   a. **GOTO**
   b. **GOSSIP**
   c. **GOSUB**

3. A subroutine must end with:
   a. quotation marks
   b. **RETURN**
   c. **END**

4. After the **GOSUB** command, there is always a:
   a. line number
   b. subroutine
   c. periscope

5. The **REM** stands for:
   a. Rapid Eye Movement
   b. Remedy
   c. Remark

6. A program is limited to one subroutine only: True or False?

11 WHAT'S NEXT?

Computers in the future

The day we were scheduled to begin our last chapter, we returned to the library. Mrs. Klemford was there and gave us a friendly nod.

"Hello, there," she warbled. "How is the book coming along?"

"Just fine," we informed her. "As a matter of fact, we're here to get some ideas for our last chapter. Do you know of any books that might describe the use of computers in the future?"

Mrs. Klemford rubbed her chin for a moment while she mentally scanned all the books in the collection.

"Ah yes," she brightened. "There is a book with just that title. Follow me."

She led us to the science and technology section and within seconds had located a book entitled "The Use of Computers in the Future."

"There you go," she said, obviously quite pleased with herself. "This ought to help you. Good luck."

With that she scurried off to see if she could find any other patrons in need of her assistance.

We quickly opened the book, eager to examine its contents. As we skimmed the first chapter, several passages jumped out at us.

"Someday computers will be small enough to comfortably fit in an office. Because of the cooling equipment necessary to keep computers at optimum operating temperatures, however, it is unlikely that they will ever find their way into the home in this century. But then what would individuals do with their own computers anyway?"

What was going on here? This passage didn't sound like an extremely foresighted vision of the future. It sounded more like a wet meteorologist forecasting fair skies.

A glance at the book's copyright date immediately cleared our confusion. Mrs. Klemford had given us a book that had been written in 1952. Oh, well. Now we were back at the point where we started.

After searching the shelves and failing to find anything better, we decided that maybe we had been looking in the wrong section. If we couldn't find what we wanted in the science books, maybe we would have better luck with science fiction.

Traversing the library, we arrived at the science fiction stacks. In addition to the many books there, we found something else.

Against the back wall was a very promising-looking door bearing the sign "The Future of Computing." (Now we know you're thinking that the likelihood of this happening twice is highly improbable, but please consider that there aren't that many different ways to get transported into another time.)

Anyway, since we now knew the score with these time portals, we opened the door and walked right into the future.

COMPUTERS IN THE HOME

We walked down a tree-lined residential street. Finding out how people were using computers in their homes would necessitate gaining entrance into somebody's home. Unfortunately, we didn't know anyone who lived here.

Figuring the truth just might work, we chose a likely-looking home and approached it. The first thing we noticed when we pressed the button mounted on the front door was the lack of chimes. Instead, a voice issued forth from a speaker, greeted us cordially, and asked us our names.

Something about the voice's diction and delivery made us think that it was strange. After a few seconds of silence, the voice came back.

"Thank you for waiting. I was just correlating your voice patterns with those in my memory."

We were being greeted by a computer! We were speechless, but the voice continued.

"I have concluded that I have never had the pleasure of meeting either of you before."

Regaining our composure, we hesitantly told the voice that the pleasure was all ours.

"As you wish," conceded the voice. "And what is the purpose of your visit?"

"We are travellers from the past," we admitted. "We are doing research for a book. We came to see how computers will be used in homes, schools, and places of business."

We realized it all sounded very farfetched, but who knows? Any society with computerized gatekeepers might readily accept the notion of time travel.

The talking computer quickly performed a stress analysis on our voices.

"You are telling the truth," it announced. "You may enter."

The door was opened by a pleasant-looking woman.

"Hello. I am Marna VI," she announced with a fastidious English accent. "I understand that you are interested in learning about the domestic use of computers."

"That's correct," we answered. "This looks like quite a place. We'd really appreciate it if someone could show us around."

"The humans are not at home at this time," Marna explained. "The adults are at work and the children are at school. I am unoccupied at the moment, and I would be pleased to guide you through the premises.

"One of my duties is that of the hardware maintenance supervisor, responsible for the well being of the computers here. I would therefore be a logical choice as I am the most capable of answering any of your questions."

In the Kitchen

After we walked through the hallway, the first room we entered was the kitchen. It was bright and clean. Every surface was either polished wood or tile and the entire room sparkled with the superhuman touch of a perfectionist.

The plants hanging in the windows were flourishing under a strictly-adhered-to watering and feeding schedule. The family dog's food and water bowls were equally well tended.

"I have read that, in the past, female humans spent much of their time in the kitchen. Is this accurate?" Marna asked us.

"Yes," we told her. "And after many centuries, they began to resent it."

"There no longer exists such cause for resentment," Marna explained. "Since food management can be so time-consuming, it is a perfect computer function. In this home, all meals are programmed months in advance. This includes every step of the process from purchasing to storing, from defrosting to cooking and serving.

"When the week's menus are being reviewed on the kitchen computer's screen, the food preparer (who may be android like me, or human) has the option of altering any menu. When a menu is decided upon, the computer checks the food storage inventory and displays a list of all items necessary for the menu and missing from storage."

"Who does the shopping?" we wanted to know.

"Shopping?"

Marna frowned slightly as she tried to recall the meaning of the word. After a brief pause, she brightened a bit and said, "The practice of going to the store and buying things was abandoned years ago. Today, the food preparer simply tells the computer to 'call up' all stores within a 10-kilometer radius and display the comparative prices for the items to be purchased.

"Orders are placed via computer link to each store and money transactions are orchestrated via bank computer to store. No one needs to 'shop' because the store delivers the food items to the home."

"That sure must save a lot of gas," we commented.

"Fossil fuels were replaced by marine-extracted hydrogen cells at the beginning of this century," Marna reported.

"How about that?" we muttered to ourselves. "Back to the computers. Marna, can you tell us what happens to the food after it arrives?"

"When the delivery has been made," she continued, "the preparer enters the kitchen with the purchased food, each item is reference-coded, and the food inventory is updated. When a meal is to be prepared, the food preparer simply enters the menu number into the computer, and all ingredients are conveyed to the food preparation area.

"The actual combining of ingredients may be done automatically or, if the food preparer is feeling a culinary urge, manually (or androidally)."

"Remarkable," was the only comment we could manage as we followed her out of the kitchen.

How Your Garden Does Grow

Through sliding glass doors adjacent to the kitchen, we walked into the greenhouse. The fruits, vegetables, and herbs there were grown hydroponically and their water and nutrient levels were managed by the garden computer.

Since light is vital to plant growth, it too was monitored by computer. Even on cloudy days the computer was able, we learned, to supply light to the plants. This was possible because the heating and cooling system of the entire house was supplied by solar energy.

If the day was bright, all excess energy was stored. Then, when the sun didn't shine, the stored energy was channeled to illuminate the greenhouse. These light and temperature fluctuations were monitored and compensated for by the garden computer and thus the growing season of these plants was endless.

Marna had recently installed a new peripheral of which she was very proud. She proceeded to tell us all about it.

"With this new adjunct to the garden computer, the computer will determine harvest time—the moment when each fruit and vegetable has reached its optimal nutritional level," she explained. "Since each plant is numbered and each fruit on the plant is also numbered, there will never be any confusion as to which fruit should be picked. The computer determines the time by analyzing data relating to the fruit's sugar content."

We couldn't help but think of the sour strawberries we had recently plucked from our own backyard plants. Recalling their taste, we winced involuntarily.

"During certain times of the day, the overhead skylights are opened so that bees and other pollinating insects can make contact with the plants."

"Do you have a way to handle garden pests?" we asked, figuring that technology must have advanced past dangerous pesticides.

"Certainly," Marna assured us. "The computer monitors the plants for the presence of pests and eliminates any it finds with pinpoints of laser light. With the tireless help of a computer, the resultant yields of this garden are enough for the family to be self-sufficient in many food items."

Anyone for a Game of...

From the garden we ventured into the family room, which was really a family entertainment center. It was by far the most impressive room in the house. Although the furniture was comfortable and inviting by old century standards, technology was visible everywhere.

"This is great!" we said, feeling like kids in a toy store. "This is the kind of room every home should have."

"The humans certainly do enjoy the time they spend here," Marna agreed. "Although it is not readily apparent, everything within this environment is controlled by computer. This includes the room's lighting, temperature, sound, and olfactory input. Any environmental mood can be created by a series of commands to the computer."

Marna revealed, with no small amount of pride and affection, that the children of the family were quite inventive when it came to creating environments.

"They derive much pleasure, for example, from mixing cool blue-white light flecks with the sound of Christmas carols and then projecting a beach scene complete with sea gull cries and the smell of ocean air."

With the push of a few buttons, she gave us a demonstration. There we

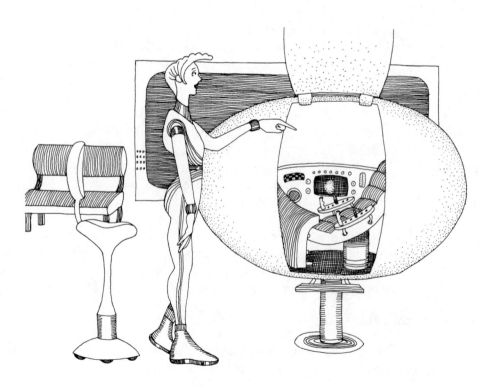

were, surrounded by the smell of popcorn and circus animals while the projected scene was a flower-laden dell complete with the twitterings of birds.

We laughed at the absurdity of it and concluded that computers were absolutely incomparable for enabling one to experience the improbable.

As might be expected, the entertainment room also included the latest in computer game technology. Players entered egg-like enclosures and completely engulfed themselves in multimedia fantasy environments.

The environments were complete in every detail, with full color, three-dimensional holography, motion control, and quadraphonic sound as standard. The players were projected into the playing field and experienced environmental changes brought about by decisions they made during the course of the game.

These simulations were so real and engrossing that the old entertainment of watching television had, along with boxing, passed into the annals of antiquity.

Marna told us that, for these humans, there was nothing more entertaining and stimulating than programming a new game simulation for the enjoyment of the family.

Now I Lay Me Down To Sleep

As we reluctantly left the entertainment center, we walked down a plushly carpeted corridor that led to a sound-cushioned section of the house. This was where each family member reposed at the end of the day. The sleeping chambers contained the same computerized light, temperature, and communications controls that were present in other rooms of the house.

"What are those devices beside the bed?" we wondered out loud.

"The larger one is an individual, programmable 'Sleep Think' computer," Marna responded. "It serves a purpose similar to the 'listen and learn while you sleep' audio devices that enjoyed some limited popularity during the twentieth century. 'Sleep Think' allows the body to rest while the computer continuously monitors receptive brain waves and transmits information directly to the sleeper.

"With a memory link to the World Library, the sleeper has access to all recorded knowledge, and can choose to learn about anything in the known universe. In addition, 95.675% retention levels are attained during this process."

Although we had never dabbled in the learning-by-osmosis technique to which Marna referred, it sounded like "Sleep Think" was ever so much more efficient.

"And what is the other thing for?" we asked, pointing to the smaller device that also sat on the night table beside the bed.

"That is 'Sleep View.' It is a computer subscription device hooked up to the ever-changing Cosmic Library of Visual Images.

"Using the 'Sleep View' menu, a sleeper can program his dreams and thus broaden his horizons by consciously directing out-of-the-body travel.

"The range of available experiences is infinite," Marna pointed out. "And this form of travel is extremely cost-effective."

As we concluded our tour, Marna asked if she could give us any other assistance in our research.

"Can you get us into a school around here?" we ventured. "We'd love to see how computers are being used in education."

"That will be no problem at all. The school attended by the children in this family is not far from here, and it follows an elaborate computer curriculum.

"Also, if you would like, I can arrange for you to visit Stephen's office. He works for a manufacturing company that is quite advanced in its use of computers."

We told her that anything she could do would be greatly appreciated. With that, Marna excused herself, promising to return shortly.

Within five minutes she returned with a piece of paper in her hand.

"You have an appointment with Claudia Bennet, an eighth grade teacher at the children's school. Later this afternoon, Stephen's employer, Ms. Gale, will be happy to meet with you in her office. Here are directions to each place. You shouldn't have any problems, they are both within walking distance."

We started to thank her for all of her help when a high-pitched sound was heard. It caused an involuntary look of concern to cross Marna's otherwise placid facade.

She quickly headed down the hall to a side room, beckoning us to follow. This relatively small room contained a master control panel with a light indicator for each one of the 32 computers in the house. A flashing red light signaled that computer number 17, located in the northwest corner of the entertainment room, had a problem.

Marna let us know in no uncertain terms that, although she had everything under control, our visit was over because she had work to do.

We thanked her again and took our leave, realizing stupidly that we had forgotten to take notes during the tour. We sincerely hoped for the sake of our publisher that our noncomputerized memory was still functioning.

THE LITTLE ELECTRONIC SCHOOL HOUSE

After leaving Marna and the computerized home of her humans, we set forth to explore the educational world and see how computers were making their influence felt there. From our first step over the threshold of Sky Skipper Middle School, we could feel that the school of the future was much changed because of the presence of computers.

The first computer in evidence sat in a prominent location in the school's lobby. As students passed by in the morning, the computer recognized and recorded each one's name. In this way attendance was taken, and calls were automatically placed to absent students so that they could receive their class assignments from the school's main computer.

Although school attendance was optional, group electives such as environmental configurations, dolphin speech analysis, and space colony preparation were so stimulating that most children greatly enjoyed coming to school.

Upon approaching the computer at the reception desk, we were asked which staff person we wished to see. When we replied, the computer screen displayed a floor plan of the school with a circle indicating Ms. Bennet's classroom.

Since we are famous for our inability to remember instructions, we requested a hard copy of the floor plan. The reception computer instantaneously obliged and printed out a map that clearly marked the path to our destination.

When we reached Room 12, we were pleasantly surprised. The children of Claudia Bennet's eighth grade class were the most enthusiastic students we had ever encountered. Even though it was spring and children their age are notorious for an inability to keep their minds on anything vaguely academic, the excitement generated by discovering and learning was in the air.

The adults in the room were not very easy to spot because the traditional configuration of a teacher's desk flanked by row upon row of student desks was missing. Instead, students were scattered everywhere around the room and each was working alone or with a partner at a small desk-top computer.

With a little searching, we managed to spot Ms. Bennet, and went over to introduce ourselves. She was extremely cordial and assured us that her students enjoyed the opportunity to show their work to visitors.

As Claudia, which she urged us to call her, showed us around the room, she explained that mornings were devoted to computer study and afternoons to electives. This morning the room was humming with computer enthusiasm.

In fact, we felt slightly overwhelmed by the high level of activity. At first glance it appeared as if everything was in a state of chaos, with students barely containing their excitement over each new entry into the computer and the computers themselves filling the room with graphic flashes and an electronic cacophony.

On closer examination of the situation, however, we saw that there was a great sense of order and purpose in the activities of the students. Each child was deeply engrossed in a programming project and the intensity with which the students worked was most admirable.

We were delighted at the sight of 20 intelligent and energetic children working with such fervor and dedication. (With great pain and suffering did we contrast and recall our own educational experience, which often included the deliverance of pedagogical commands such as, "Everyone open your math books to page 178.")

Here were individuals using computers to think and create as individuals. As a result, the variety of projects in the creation process was a marvel to behold.

"Do you have a particular area of interest?" Claudia asked after we had become accustomed to the room and what was going on there.

"Maybe you could show us some of the special things that the children have programmed by themselves," we suggested.

With that she scanned the group for a moment and then led us over to a curly-haired plump girl sitting in front of a computer.

"This is Natasha," Claudia began. "She is one of our newer students. She is programming a synthesized symphony."

Natasha barely noticed us standing over her, as she was quite busy composing and conducting. When she did glance up, she giggled and modestly asked, "Would you like to see what I'm working on?"

Our eager nods encouraged her to talk a bit about the stereo sound track she was programming for her own computer-animated cartoon. As if by way of apology, she warned us, "Don't expect too much because I just moved to

this district last year and my old school had a different kind of computer."

Despite the false modesty (because she really was a very talented programmer), Natasha proudly showed us what she had accomplished in the two weeks since she had begun the project.

By commanding the computer to commence the program, she showed us her own version of the life cycle of a monarch butterfly. The smooth flow of the animation that she had been able to accomplish was truly impressive. The lovely images were produced in great detail and the available palette of 16 million colors and shades rivaled nature.

As a finishing touch to her computer-generated creation, Natasha was working on blending sounds from a fully synthesized orchestra. The tones would ebb and flow as a dramatic accompaniment to the vivid images on the screen. We were astonished by the beauty of her work.

"That was the most beautiful thing we've ever seen on a computer," we told her. "We would love to come back and experience the whole thing when you are done."

Natasha blushed with pleasure and went back to her program.

Geoffry was a small, bespectacled boy sitting at the next table. Claudia explained that Geoffry was working on an astronomy simulation.

"For his program," she explained, "Geoffry has chosen to simulate the star field that includes the constellation Cassiopeia. He is currently programming the location of each star, planet, and asteroid.

"His goal is to create a computer program that will, from any planetary viewpoint, display the movement of each celestial body across the sky as well as the luminance variation of each star. Did I describe that accurately, Geoffry?"

"Uh, huh," an engrossed Geoffry responded, his hands never leaving the keyboard. "Ultimately, I want this program to also include the predictable occurrences of novas and black holes and a light speed journey through the field. I think I have a way to go before it can do that!"

He chuckled to himself as he continued his work.

We soon saw that not all of the computer work in Claudia Bennet's class was being done at keyboards. Two students nearby seemed to be talking to their computer. And what a strange-looking computer it was, complete with appendages and an agile "hand" with thumb-forefinger opposition.

"What are those two doing?" we wanted to know.

"Carolyn and Richard are programming a voice-activated computer," Claudia told us.

"Their current voice programming task, which they dreamed up themselves, is the isolation of the 375 different actions involved in troubleshooting and repairing the propulsion mechanism on a motorized skateboard."

"How's it going, kids?" we asked.

"Pretty well," Richard answered. "We almost have it so that it can distinguish between the blodget nut and the wicket screw."

"When we have this program perfected," Carolyn explained, "we're going to open a skateboard repair shop somewhere near the school."

Though impressed by their youthful ingenuity, we had to move on.

"Are any of the kids doing anything with foreign languages?" we asked Claudia.

"As a matter of fact, I was just going to show you our computerized foreign language lab."

In a soundproof room within a room, children in enclosed cubicles were learning foreign languages from the synthesized voices of computers. It was quite an extraordinary sight.

Each computer, sounding like a native of the student's chosen country, would engage the student in conversation. Then, as the student responded to the computer's questions, the computer would analyze the student's voice and correct the diction and accent.

"This program has been extremely valuable," Claudia said. "And since becoming literate in a foreign language also involves a knowledge of grammar and syntax, these verbal foreign language sessions are always used in conjuction with learning sessions from the home's 'Sleep Think' computer."

"This certainly makes a lot more sense than 30 kids with terrible accents saying, 'Bonjour, Madame Dupont,' " we laughed.

"Oh yes," Claudia agreed. "In fact, this method is so successful that it is not uncommon for a child to become fluent in a new language every month."

A sudden explosion of gleeful shouts directed our attention to yet another portion of the room.

"What's happening over there?" we asked.

Claudia told us that the students who were having so much fun were involved in a specialized remedial math program. (How many times did we laugh in all the hours we practiced our multiplication tables?)

"In fact," she continued, "the computer programs these students are using to help reinforce their math skills are delightful economic simulations that were programmed by the accelerated math students of the school. These simulations help the students internalize math concepts that they missed in the earlier grades."

Claudia also told us that these games, with names like "Bendiltrix Corp," "Lollipop Factory," and "Space Shuttle Showroom," were giving the students an opportunity to take the role of management, labor, or consumer and learn about math by interacting with the economic system.

"The computer acts as stockbroker, banker, and financial consultant," Claudia added, "and requires that the student really understand the rules of the math and money game before making any decisions."

It sure sounded like fun, and the kids obviously thought so too!

Our visit was drawing to an end. The morning work period was over and Ms. Bennet informed the kids that it was almost lunch time. With great sighs and groans the students grudgingly put the final touches on their work, saved the revised programs on microdisks (wafer-thin magnetic storage media the size of a quarter), turned off their computers, and cleared out of the room.

We thanked Claudia and told her how much we had enjoyed the visit. It really had been a pleasure to bask in the creative energy of her students.

As we said our goodbyes and walked down the street, we mused to ourselves about the creative potential that was being unleashed in Claudia's classroom. This was one place where the computer helped to make learning fantastically fun, and, because of it, school wasn't drudgery.

Those kids were great, we thought as we departed. They certainly gave the computers a workout, and vice versa.

COMPUTERS IN THE WORK PLACE

To round out our visit to the future we went to the corporate headquarters of TwindleBeds, Inc., the company that employed Stephen, Marna's human.

Upon entering the massive building, we were greeted by a pleasant-looking man with a warm handshake.

"Hello, I'm Stephen. Marna told me that you folks are doing some special research on computers."

"That's right," we told him. "And we certainly learned a lot at your house and at your children's school."

"Good." Stephen seemed pleased. "Now let me send you in to meet my boss and see if she can give you some information about how we use computers here in our operation."

Glenda Gale, the president of TwindleBeds, sat behind her oak desk as we entered her spacious office. Like the others we had visited, she was happy to help us with our research.

Her eyes glistened with the prospect of having her company written up in a book. With a directness that often marks an executive, she invited us in and proceeded to tell us the details about her fully computerized business.

"In our company, computers have taken over all of the most menial and repetitive of tasks," explained Ms. Gale. "This includes inventory, accounts payable and receivable, ordering of raw materials, assembly of parts, quality control, new orders, and payroll.

"This leaves the humans free to work at all of the really creative aspects of the business—new products design, promotional materials, and customer relations.

"Although several labor groups were wary when the computers started coming in here, the truth is, our production has increased so much that our payroll now supports three times the number of people it did before we computerized our operation.

"Since all of the computer functions I mentioned are fully automated and require only sporadic human monitoring, I imagine you would be more interested in interactions that take place between humans and computers."

"You are right. That's just what we would like to hear about," we assured her.

"Let's look at word processing, for example," she continued. "Although it is hardly a new use of computers, we here at TwindleBeds have a voice-activated word processor that far excels the capabilities of the old-fashioned touch model.

"This device allows me to dictate letters, interoffice memoranda, and so on, directly into the computer. Then Stephen reviews the text and, since he has a literary editor's way with words, tidies things up.

"Later, I call up the revision and either approve it or make some more changes. When the final text is composed, it is stored on the computer's laser disk.

"In the case of letters to board members, Stephen will instruct the computer to electronically 'mail' a copy of each letter along with any relevant graphs and charts to each director. By this, of course, I mean that the text of the letter is transmitted directly from our computer to each director's computer."

"And how do you use computers in the designing of new products?" we queried.

To this Ms. Gale quickly responded, "Our computers help our designers by first analyzing individual market trends within each of our 47 regional areas. These trends give us an excellent indication of consumer bed preferences.

"Once the data are analyzed, we are able to design exactly what the consumers in each region most want in a bed. And at that point it's over to the computer drawing board, so to speak.

"Actually, our drawing board consists of a computer with full three-dimensional color graphics capabilities," she went on. "Based on the specifications that our designers input, the drawing of the bed emerges.

"Before the actual bed is constructed, the proposed design is fit into a computer-generated display of a bedroom, complete with carpeting and a specific motif. This way there are never any surprises when our robot assembly line gives the bed a three-dimensional life in physical space.

"We have already verified the bed's attractiveness in specific environments. In addition, we always know we have a durable product because the

computer-generated model can be subjected to all kinds of pressure and tension tests.

"When the computer model is complete, its plan is sent down to the robots in the factory and they construct the prototype. If everything goes well, and it does 99% of the time, we are ready to go into full production of a new TwindleBeds bed."

With the last phrase still resonating in the room, Glenda Gale smiled the smile of a satisfied person. "The creation of a new product is as easy as that," she said matter-of-factly. "Currently, we have 225 different models for sale."

Ms. Gale, perceptive creature that she was, could hardly fail to notice our utter astonishment at the mention of so many different types of beds. She nodded knowingly and said, "You are obviously wondering how in the cosmos we are able to effectively produce that many different beds. I'll tell you.

"It's as easy for our robot assembly computers to remember how to build 225 models as it is to remember the plans for five.

"Of course, it would probably overwhelm the average consumer to have to choose from that many possibilities, so our regional catalogs only include those models which our market data tell us are viable choices in each region."

That sounded very logical to us.

"When it comes to advertising our beds," Ms. Gale continued, "the computer is, once again, indispensable. We here at TwindleBeds believe that a bed is not just a bed, but a part of one's home.

"It is essential that the consumer envision the bed he is about to buy in this way too.

"When a consumer is shopping for beds, he can call our computer and superimpose the computer-generated image of any bed he likes onto the three-dimensional image of his sleeping chamber stored in his own home computer.

"In this way, the bed is always shown off to its fullest advantage. The consumer sees not just a product in isolation, but a living integral part of his home, something that he can live with comfortably for many years."

At that moment, a beep sounded and Ms. Gale begged our pardon and switched on her desk monitor. Stephen's voice and face appeared instantly.

"Excuse me, Ms. Gale," he said. "Higgins is waiting for your review of the new mercury flotation suspension design."

"Thank you, Stephen," she said as she clicked off the monitor. Turning to us, she added, "I really must be going. I hope this has been of value to your research."

We assured her that it most certainly had.

She thanked us for coming, escorted us to the door, and with a parting glance said, "I hope you don't mind my saying this, but the way you hold your neck to the side like that is a prime indication that the bed you're sleeping on is just not right for you. Why don't you take this copy of our catalog disk with you?"

Even though we weren't in the market for a bed, she was rather insistent, so we thanked her and took the disk. It would make interesting viewing back in the present—that is, if we could find the right kind of disk drive in which to use it.

Our research completed, we knew that it was time to return. Like seasoned travellers, we had no trouble finding the door this time. Upon opening it and entering the library, we found everything as we had expected.

On our way home, we realized that we still had the catalog disk from

TwindleBeds. We became excited by what it could mean to have information directly from the future. We mused over the possibilities at dinner. Perhaps, if we began tinkering with a few circuit boards, we could push the technology forward a little faster. And if we could do that, we just might beat Ms. Gale in founding a multimillion dollar, computer-designed bed business. Sipping the last of our coffee, we agreed that it certainly was an interesting thought.

EPILOGUE

The early morning rays peeked over the windowsill of Fred Frantic's computer room. If the sunlight hadn't literally hit him in the eye he would have barely noticed that a new day had dawned. The sun often found him here, before the rest of the street was awake. And although it could hardly understand why this particular human would sacrifice the sleep that so many others craved, it had to admit he seemed to be enjoying himself.

Fred stood up, stretched, and reluctantly reached over and switched off his computer.

"I can't believe I worked through another night!" Fred marveled with amusement. "This computer stuff is absolutely addictive. I don't even consider this work. I, who was always the first one out of the office door at 5, now work all hours just for the fun of it."

"Just for the fun of it" was not exactly an accurate description of what Fred was doing, although it is obvious that it felt like that to him.

A year and a half had passed since his first scary encounter at the computer store, and he had come a long way since then. He had bought a computer, not with total confidence, but with a feeling of optimism. He had subscribed to a few computer magazines, learned the terminology, and purchased several simple game programs so his computer wouldn't get hungry. He discovered to his utter delight that he really enjoyed the time he spent with the computer, but after a week or two he felt that he wanted to do more.

"This computer stuff is fascinating. I can't get enough of it. And I'll bet it would be even more interesting if I could learn to write my own programs. After all," he had reasoned, "it's my computer. I ought to be able to talk to it myself."

So Fred undertook the task of teaching himself BASIC. He took a course at the local computer center and bought himself a good beginner's book. At the end of eighteen months the man was flying. It was as if he had been born to program. His software was being marketed through a national publishing house, and for the first time in his life he was thinking of himself as a creative person. The best part of it was that his monthly royalty checks were bringing in more than his office job ever had.

With this feeling of pride and a sense of well-being, he went into the kitchen to make himself some breakfast. The day was bright, and Fred found himself dreaming of his next program as he scrambled the eggs. He was awakened from his reverie by the telephone.

"Hello."

"How are you doing, Fred? It's Martin. Didn't wake you up, did I?"

"No, not at all," Fred chuckled, glancing at the clock. Six A.M. It always amused him that Martin, with all his computer prowess, never could remember that there was a three-hour time difference between his new neighborhood and his old one.

"What's new with you, old buddy?" Martin wanted to know. "It's been a long time."

"I'm just fine. You'd be interested in knowing that I bought a computer a while back."

"You? No kidding? That's really a coincidence. Why, I was just looking at the latest issue of *Computers Today* and saw an advertisement for a program called Datawhiz. And the author's name was Fred Frantic. I immediately thought of you, of course, and how ironic it was that someone named Fred Frantic was writing programs. No offense, old buddy, but from my experience that name is certainly not synonymous with computers!"

"That's my program, Martin," Fred said proudly.

After Martin had recovered his senses, Fred filled him in on the beautiful relationship that had developed between him and his computer. For the next half hour the friends chatted away about RAM and ROM and the comparative graphics capabilities of their respective computers.

"Well, I'm really proud of you, Fred," Martin said with genuine affection. "It sounds like you're doing just great, and I couldn't be happier. In fact, it sure would be terrific if two computer buffs like us could live a little closer to each other. That way we could really spend some time together. You know, this may sound crazy, but the house across the street is up for sale. Think you might be interested in making a move?"

Fred looked out the window at his front yard and smiled.

QUIZ ANSWERS

Answers to Chapter 2 Quiz

1. *b*—Silicon, the main ingredient in microprocessors, is found in sand.
2. *c*—Human memory is a massive tangle of information.
3. *c*—Random Access Memory, the "write on" and "read from" portion of the computer's memory.
4. *c*—K stands for kilo, or thousand, so 24K means 24 thousand.
5. *False*—It may be floppy but it's definitely *not* flabby.
6. *d*—Sorry, as yet there is no known way of connecting a tennis racquet to a computer.

Answers to Chapter 3 Quiz

1. *d*—BASIC (Beginner's All-purpose Symbolic Instruction Code) is the only real one on this list.

2. *a*—When given a **PRINT** command followed by a string enclosed in quotes, the computer will always respond by **PRINT**ing the string.

3. *False*—The only way a computer can treat numbers as numbers is if they are *not* enclosed in quotation marks.

4. *c*—The command **NEW** is the only one that will clear the memory. If you try *a*, *b*, or *d*, the computer will chuckle and say **SYNTAX ERROR**.

5. *b*—Better not forget your line numbers if you want your commands to be remembered by the computer.

6. *b*—A line number must be a *whole number* (no decimals allowed).

7. *c*—You can always correct a line by reentering it using the same line number.

8. *d*—To delete a line just type the number of the line and press **RETURN**. Choice *a* (**NEW**) would also have deleted Line 40 but it would have taken the rest of the program with it.

9. *a*—The answer **LIST** tells the computer to display all the BASIC commands currently stored in memory.

10. *d*—Bernard Baruch was philanthropic, the Tin Woodsman was sentimental, and a mule is obstinate. But we've never met a computer that was any of these.

Answers to Chapter 4 Quiz

1. *c*—The last character of a string variable name is always a dollar sign ($).

2. Answers *a* and *c* are correct. Answers *b* and *d* could not be string variable names because they lack a dollar sign.

3. *Line 30* is the proper way to assign a value to a string variable.

4. *a*—In most BASICs, semicolons are used to separate variables from text in a **PRINT** statement.

Printout of final program in Chapter 4:

```
Dear Miranda Veranda,

    Congratulations, Miranda Veranda,
we are delighted to tell you about a
special prize which is coming to you
at your home on 123 Willowood Road.
Yes, you and your canary, who will
soon celebrate his number 2 year on
this planet, will be receiving a 350
pound bag of Wonderpet canary food.

    Again, our heartfelt congratula-
tions to you, Miranda Veranda, and
may you and your canary enjoy
another 100 happy years together.



Sincerely,
Wonderpet Food Company
```

5. *b*—Dollar signs are used only for string variables. Letters and numbers are permitted as part of any variable name.

6. *b*—Dollar signs and commas are characters and therefore cannot be placed in a numeric variable.

   c—Sorry, Emily, numeric variables are reserved only for numbers.

   d—This value could be placed in a numeric variable, but you would get the result of 555 *minus* 1212, or -657, instead of a phone number. A hyphen and a minus sign (-) are the same character on the keyboard, but this character will always be interpreted by the computer as a minus sign when it appears outside of quotation marks.

7. *Lines 10, 20,* and *40* are fine. *Line 30* has an error because the string (Pshaw!) needs quotation marks around it.

8. *d*—That's how they do it!

9. Answers *a* and *d* are acceptable names for numeric variables. Both **PLANT$** and **FOOD$** are string variable names, but **LETTER** won't work because it contains **LET**, a reserved word.

10. *b*—You can always change the value in a variable by rewriting the **LET** statement. Answer *c* would work too but it would cause you to lose your whole program.

11. *c*—Since **NUMBER** is a numeric variable, it can only contain a number. Answer *b* is incorrect because the contents of numeric variables are never enclosed in quotes.

12. *True*—Sure they can. See our preceding "Dear Miranda" program.

13. *d*—A **LET** statement stores something in a box; the **PRINT** statement displays (unveils) it on the screen.

Answers to Chapter 5 Quiz

1. *c*—Although it would be nice if it could do some of those other things.

2. *a*—Because, like clay, **INPUT** is flexible.

3. *Line 20*—The command is **INPUT** not **IMPUT**.

   Lines 50 and 60—The entry **PLACE** needs to be **PLACE$** because the answer to the question is going to include words.

4. *True*—There's no reason why not.

5. *c*—Remember, **GOTO** always activates a **GOTO** loop, telling the computer to return to the specified line number.

6. *a*—The interrupt key will break into any program instantly without destroying any of the information in the computer's memory.

7. *b*—The variable in an **INPUT** statement is always an answer box, never an answer.

   d—Don't bother with question marks; usually a free one comes with every **INPUT** statement.

8. *a*

9. *d*—That question would require a yes or no answer and we haven't learned how to respond to one of those yet.

10. *Line 80*—We need a string variable to store the answer to the salad dressing question.

Answers to Chapter 6 Quiz

1. *c*—T-H-E-N is the only acceptable way to spell **THEN**.

2. *Line 20* is incorrect because **ANSWER$** cannot equal 1750 (if it did, it would have to be a numeric variable and not a string variable). Lines 10 and 30 are just fine the way they are.

3. *b*—A colon (:) is what you must place at the end of any statement to which you would like to add another statement.

4. *a*—Only one condition needs to be true in an **IF/THEN** statement that uses **OR**. Answer *c* would be correct if you were using **AND** in an **IF/THEN** statement. Answer *b* is correct when discussing a majority vote in Congress.

5. *b*—Computers are so jaded that they are never impressed by anything.

6. *False*—The "less than" symbol points to the left. (Remember the letter "l" for less and left.)

7. *a*—"less than"
   c—"greater than"
   d—"equals"
   e—"not equal to"
   All of the preceding answers are fine for use in conditional statements. Answer *b*, the exclamation point, would mean nothing to the computer if it were not part of a string enclosed in quotes.

Answers to Chapter 7 Quiz

1. *c*—The **FOR/NEXT** loop is used to repeat tasks a certain number of times.

2. Within a single loop, **FOR** always comes *before* **NEXT**. By reversing Lines 10 and 30, the program would be fine.

3. *True*—Sure it can. Refer back to each program in this chapter for verification.

4. *Line 30*—You don't end a **FOR/NEXT** loop with the word **ANOTHER**, you end it with the word **NEXT**.

5. *Line 10*—And it would be rewritten to look like this:
   ```
   10 FOR LOOP = 1 TO 7
   ```

6. *b*—That is the only correct syntax. Answer *a* is incorrect because the variable in a **FOR/NEXT** loop can never be a *string* variable. Answer *c* is incorrect because a **FOR/NEXT** loop requires the word **TO** between two numbers, not a dash (—).

Answers to Chapter 8 Quiz

1. *b*—The command
   ```
   R = INT(RND(1) * 10 + 1)
   ```
   will result in the computer randomly picking a whole number between 1 and 10.

2. Answers *a*, *b*, and *d* can be programmed with the random number formula because they are simulations of random events. Most people's checkbook expenditures are not random.

3. *d*—The abbreviation **INT** means integer, or "whole number," and is seen in the random number formula.

4. *c*—Two pairs is correct. See answer to Question 1.

5. *b*—The formula will yield any whole number from 1 to 1000.

6. *c*—No matter how fancy your programming skills become, **PRINT** is still the most straightforward way to get something displayed on the screen.

Answers to Chapter 9 Quiz

1. *c*—Whenever you need a quick way to put a series of values into a variable, remember **READ/DATA**.

2. *b*—The **FOR/NEXT** loop is set to the same number as the number of pieces of data on the data line.

3. *Line 40*—There is no BASIC command **NIX**.
   Line 50—Individual pieces of data on a **DATA** line are always separated by commas. (The quotes are optional in most BASICs.)

4. *True*—Data on a **DATA** line can be anything.

5. *a*—The **READ** command is the only BASIC command to unlock the secrets of the **DATA** line.

6. Answer *b* (in some BASICs) and answer *c* are both correct.

7. *d*—One of the few times in our quizzes when "all of the above" is actually the right answer.

Answers to Chapter 10 Quiz

1. *b*—A subroutine is a line (or series of lines) within a program that performs a certain task within the context of the entire program.

2. *c*—The command **GOSUB** is the only *legal* way to call up a subroutine.

3. *b*—The entry **RETURN** must be present at the end of a subroutine. It's like a roundtrip ticket. Without it you'll never get home again. As for answer *c*, **END** can be used as the command that separates the subroutine from the rest of the program.

4. *a*—You can't tell the computer to **GOSUB** if you don't tell it *where* the subroutine is. That's why you need a line number.

5. *a*—Rapid Eye Movement is correct if you're discussing dreams and sleep cycles.
   c—Remark is the correct translation of **REM** into BASIC.

6. *False*—The number of subroutines in a single program is unrestricted.

GLOSSARY

The basics of computer terminology

When in the company of colleagues, computer people, like physicians, lawyers, and musicians, often revert to a jargon that is fraught with meaning for them but is totally incomprehensible to the uninitiated. If you heard someone ask, "How many bytes are in your buffer?", you might be inclined to think the person was making a suggestive remark.

To enlighten you and thus help you to avoid undue embarrassment, we have provided an abridged Computerese-to-English dictionary. Here is a handy glossary of computer terms that, depending upon the circles in which you travel these days, may or may not be in evidence.

alphanumeric. The combination of letters and numbers used by a computer. For example, "1 if by land, 2 if by sea" could only have been written on an alphanumeric keyboard.

ASCII (as-key). Stands for American Standard Code for Information Interchange. A system by which each key (or combination of keys) on the keyboard has a numeric value (from 0 to 127). One of the few things that *almost* all microcomputers have in common.

backup (*verb*). The process of making a copy of a diskette or cassette so you have a spare in case something happens to the original—diskettes are favorite playthings of small dogs and children. (*noun*) The diskette or cassette copy produced above.

253

BASIC. A very popular computer language available on most microcomputers. Stands for Beginner's All-purpose Symbolic Instruction Code. For more on this wonderful language, see Chapters 3 through 10.

baud rate. The rate (in bits per second) at which information is transmitted between computer and computer or computer and peripheral. The rate 300 baud is rather slow (about 30 characters per second) and 38,400 baud is rather fast (almost 4000 characters per second). Baud rate has nothing to do with your pulse after a session of aerobic exercises.

bit. The smallest unit of computer memory, it can have a value of either 1 or 0, on or off (like a light switch). Actually one-eighth of a byte. Don't worry too much about this one. Most beginners never come face-to-face with a bit. And really, what does an eighth of a character mean anyway?

bomb (*verb*). To have a computer or program suddenly die. The unpredictable and usually extremely inconvenient demise of the electronic servant, which invariably occurs at a time when you have neglected to save the last eight hours' worth of information in your computer.

boot (*verb*). The process of turning your computer on and first loading its programs. Originates from the Protestant Ethic adage, "Virtuous is the downtrodden man who pulls himself up by his bootstraps." (*noun*) Cowboy footgear, usually comes in pairs.

bug. Anything you've got in a program (yours or somebody else's) that causes the program to do something other than what it's supposed to do. Bugs are a blight on every programmer's sense of well being. They are, by nature, insidious creatures (we're talking about the bugs now, not the programmers) and have an irritating habit of turning up just when you think that your work is done.

byte (bite). A single character of information stored in a computer's memory. In some circumstances (for example, when you are programming or using a word processor), every time you hit one of those keys on the keyboard you are unwittingly putting all your w's, q's, commas, and apostrophes into little boxes inside the subcircuit recesses of RAM. A byte is made up of eight bits (*see* bit).

cassette. A regular audio recording cassette. It can be used (with the help of a tape recorder) to store computer data. Cheap but not very reliable.

compiler. Any programming language that must send your program through an error-checking and boiling-down step before it can be executed. Compiled programs generally execute faster and take up less space than programs written with an interpreter (*see* interpreter). However, they are not interactive, so working with them is harder.

CP/M. Stands for Control Program for Microcomputers. A popular computer program that allows a computer to talk with its disk drives (for example, saving and loading programs, listing the names of the programs on the diskette, erasing programs, and so on). Used most often for business applications. It is considered fashionable to have CP/M; otherwise, it's obvious to all that you only bought your computer for game playing.

CPU. Stands for Central Processing Unit. This is the computer's "brain," the place where all calculations take place and everything is orchestrated. On microcomputers, the CPU is located on a 1/4-inch square of silicon. Computer enthusiasts expound on their CPUs the way car lovers brag about horsepower.

crash. Synonymous with bomb. When used in reference to a diskette, it also means that you lost all or part of the information stored on it.

CRT (cathode ray tube). The only vacuum tube found connected to most computers. It is the screen upon which the computer makes its wishes known to us humans.

CTRL (control). A key usually found on the lower left-hand side of a keyboard. It is pressed along with another key to give the computer a command. For example, **CTRL C** (the **CONTROL** button is held down, then "C" is pressed) acts on some computers as an emergency brake and stops the program dead in its tracks.

cursor. (1) The ever-present box or line of light on the screen—blinking or otherwise—from which all print seems to emanate (known in some circles as the Guiding Light). (2) Alternate name for a programmer whose program has just bombed.

daisy wheel. A plastic- or metal-spoked wheel that contains all the letters, numbers, and punctuation marks at the outside tips of the spokes. When used in a daisy wheel printer, it produces letter quality output.

DATA. A BASIC statement that indicates a storage place for pieces of information accessed only by a **READ** statement (*see* **READ**).

density (single/double/quad). Refers to the amount of information that can be stored on a diskette. The higher the density, the more information is packed on the diskette's surface. Double density diskettes hold twice the information as single density and half the information as "quad" density.

disk drive. The computer peripheral that reads and records information on a disk. Can refer to either a floppy or hard disk. When its red light is on, *don't* open the drive door.

diskette. Alias floppy diskette, alias floppy disk, alias floppy, alias disk, alias disc. A popular flexible magnetic storage medium used to permanently store information and programs for computers. The diskette, shaped much like a phonograph record, is sealed inside a square plastic envelope. Diskettes come in 8-inch, 5 1/4-inch, and 3-inch diameters. Interestingly enough, the diskette's physical size is no indication of how much information it can store (there are single- and double-sided diskettes as well as different densities—*see* density). Some say that airport X-ray machines are hazardous to the health of diskettes (as well as people), so take appropriate precautions.

documentation. The complete set of instructions that should accompany all computer products (hardware and software). Unfortunately, much of today's documentation is best used to line bird cages and litter boxes.

DOS (Disk Operating System). The program that allows your computer to talk with its disk drives (for example, saving and loading programs, listing the names of the programs on the diskette, erasing programs, and so on). The computer program CP/M is an example of a popular DOS.

execute. The process by which your computer follows the instructions of a program (*see* RUN). An interesting term, since "executing" a program actually brings it to life.

floppy diskette. *See* diskette.

GIGO. Garbage In, Garbage Out. Real computers don't act like most fictional computers. If you put nonsensical information into a real computer, you get nothing but nonsense back out. Since it's almost never really the computer's fault, GIGO is another way of saying, "the byte stops here."

GOSUB. (1) The BASIC statement that tells the computer to GO execute a SUBroutine. Always paired with a RETURN command (*see* RETURN, subroutine). (2) Cheers often heard during maritime maneuvers.

GOTO. The BASIC statement that tells the computer where to go. Must always be followed by a line number, the "address" to which the computer will jump. (You wouldn't want to send the computer somewhere it wasn't wanted!)

hard copy. (1) The output from a computer when printed on paper by a printer. (2) A counterfeit coin.

hard disk drive. A magnetic storage device that can hold greater amounts of information than floppy diskettes. The circular disk in most microcomputer hard disk drives is not removable (so don't try to touch it).

hardware. Any tangible equipment that comprises a computer system. For example, computer, keyboard, CRT, disk drive, printer, and so forth.

high-level language. Any computer language that enables the user to write programs using English-like words. BASIC, Pascal, LOGO, FORTH, PILOT, COBOL, FORTRAN, C, and Ada are popular high-level languages.

IF/THEN. A BASIC statement that allows the computer to appear to make decisions by comparing values (either numbers or strings). Also called a "conditional statement" because it will do something only if a condition is met (true). In other words, IF there is chocolate mousse for dessert, THEN forget about your diet and enjoy the mousse.

INPUT. The BASIC statement that allows a user (human) to enter information into a program *while the program is running*. Usually, the information is in response to questions displayed on the computer screen. (Those questions were, of course, originally created by another human known as a programmer.)

input (*noun*). The information entered into a program when requested by the computer, that is, the answer to a question. (*verb*) The act of putting in information in response to a computer-generated question.

INT. A BASIC function that will turn any decimal fraction into a whole number. It does this by returning the next lowest whole number, or integer value (hence its name). The INT function will not automatically round a number either up or down.

integer. A number without any fractional part, a whole number. If it has a decimal point, it isn't an integer. The numbers 1, 22, and 1242 are integers. The numbers 3.531, 20031.002, and 0.48 are *not*.

interpreter. A computer language that is interactive. Unlike a compiler, an interpreter allows you to enter a program and then execute it without any other steps. The language will *interpret* each line of the program as it comes to it rather than beforehand. Most microcomputers come with a BASIC interpreter (*see* compiler).

K. Stands for Kilo, which means 1000. It is used when talking about thousands of bytes (kilobytes). Remember 64,000 bytes is the same as 64K bytes, or just 64K. Actually, when referring to bytes, K means 1024 bytes.

LET. The BASIC statement that instructs the computer to create a variable (storage box) and put a specific value (a number or a string of characters) into it. The use of this statement is usually optional. For example, **ANSWER$="peanuts"** is understood by most versions of BASIC as **LET ANSWER$="peanuts."**

LIST. (1) The BASIC command that tells the computer to display on the screen the program currently in its memory. (2) Poetic form of listen.

low-level language. The computer language in which high-level languages are written. Two examples are Assembly Language and Machine Language (*see* high-level language).

memory. (1) The place where the computer stores programmed information. (2) The mental collection humans have of momentous things, like the first kiss, a trip to the Grand Canyon, or the day the family hamster died.

microcomputer. A small computer (pocket size to desk-top size). Its brain (CPU) is located on a chip (microprocessor). Usually priced somewhere between $100 and $15,000.

microprocessor. A CPU on a silicon chip. The brain of any microcomputer (*see* CPU).

modem. A peripheral device that allows your computer to use the telephone lines to call up another computer. It is used when accessing large computers that may be located across town or across the continent and have huge amounts of data.

NEW. The BASIC command that *erases* any program currently in the computer's memory, giving you a clean slate to begin again. Never use it unless you mean it.

output. The information that the computer displays on the screen. Some programmers are put out by their computer's output. But if they are, they have no one to blame but themselves. (This is a reference to the GIGO phenomenon mentioned earlier.)

parallel. A method of transferring information between a computer and its peripherals. Because the information is sent in one-byte chunks (groups of eight bits), this method of sending the data is faster than serial, which sends the information one bit at a time (*see* serial).

peripheral. Any device that can be added to a microcomputer system to expand and extend the computer's capabilities. Printers, disk drives, modems, and so forth are all peripherals, and wonderful add-ons to have if you can afford them.

PRINT. The BASIC statement given to the computer any time you want to *display* something on the screen.

printer. A peripheral that prints your listings, reports, or data on paper, much like a typewriter. Printers can range in price from $100 to $30,000, depending on the quality of print they produce and how fast they produce it.

program. A set of instructions written for a computer to follow. Programs are programmed via a keyboard by programmers.

programmer. A person often identifiable by his or her calloused fingertips and frequently muttered phrases like, "I almost have it..." or "I think it's done." In this case "it" refers to the program that this person has been writing for the past 49 hours.

RAM. Stands for Random Access Memory and represents the usable memory (measured in byte-size pieces) inside the computer. The contents of RAM vanish when the computer is turned off, so its information is usually first stored on diskette or cassette. In most cases, RAM is described in 1000-byte increments (indicated by the letter K in 16K, 64K, 128K)—*see* byte, **K**.

random. An unpredictable, unmeditated occurrence. Usually refers to the choice of a number selected as a result of the Random Number Formula, which uses BASIC's RND function. Keep in mind that, strictly speaking, the computerized selection of random numbers is seldom random (*see* RND).

READ. The BASIC statement that tells the computer to place a value from a DATA line into a variable (*see* **DATA**).

REM. The BASIC command that stands for remark and allows the programmer to interlace his or her program listing with marginal notes (that is, internal documentation), copyright information, advertisements, or whatever. The computer will never execute a **REM** statement; therefore, this backstage graffiti will never appear on the screen when the program is run.

resolution. The degree of definition with which a computer displays text, graphics, or both on the screen. The CRT's resolution is a function of the number of points of light on the screen. The more points, the higher the resolution.

RESTORE. The BASIC statement that instructs the computer to reset the **READ/DATA** "arrow" (see Chapter 10) to the beginning of the program. This means that when the **DATA** is **RESTORE**d, it can be accessed again by the computer.

RETURN. (1) The all-important button on the keyboard to be pressed *after* every command given to the computer. If **RETURN** isn't pressed, then the computer usually has not received the message. (2) The BASIC statement that marks the end of a subroutine (sent by the **GOSUB** statement) and that tells the computer to **RETURN** to the next command in the program. (3) The dreaded report that must be sent to the IRS each spring.

RND. The BASIC function that returns a decimal value between 0 and 1. Used to generate a random number (*see* random).

ROM. Stands for Read Only Memory and represents a special part of the computer's memory, a part that cannot be "written" on or erased, even when the computer is unplugged. Contains programs for the computer's minimal functioning. In some computers, the BASIC language is stored in ROM.

RS-232. The name of a standard type of cable and connector used to attach a computer to its peripherals, especially printers (used for serial data transfers—*see* serial).

RUN. The BASIC command that means "execute." Without it, a program will never get off the ground. The **RUN** command is like the gun that is fired at the starting line, the match that ignites the wood, or the avalanche that starts the rock slide.

serial. A method of transferring information between a computer and its peripherals. The information is sent across a couple of wires, one bit at a time. Because the bits are sent sequentially, one by one, rather than in groups of eight as with parallel transmission, serial is generally slower.

software. The instructions (programs) that make the computer perform its specified tasks.

string. (1) A series of characters (bytes) surrounded by quotation marks. (2) Cotton substance used by bakeries to keep you out of the cookies until you get home.

subroutine. A subprogram or module that can be used repeatedly during the execution of a program. It is accessed by the BASIC GOSUB command (*see* GOSUB).

tractor feed. (1) A sprocketed device that is connected to a printer and "feeds" the printer continuous form paper with little sprocket holes on both edges. (2) Fuel for a farm machine.

user. Any human who uses a computer. Has nothing to do with illicit drugs, although many programmers (a certain breed of users) have been known to go into withdrawal if their computers are taken away from them.

user group. A group of computer owners and potential owners who meet on a regular basis to trade information, gossip, software, and support. A great way to learn about computers. Often, there are user groups in most geographical areas for each specific brand of computer.

variable. A box in memory that can hold either a string of characters or a numeric value. Variables can be filled, emptied, compared, incremented, and otherwise manipulated. Variables rarely have any say in the matter.

word processing. The electronic manipulation of text. A word processing program in a computer enables a user to edit text in a speedy and efficient manner. This entire book was composed on a computer with word processing software.

INDEX

263